Little
Sweetheart

Little Sweetheart

*How I Was Groomed,
Abused, & Raped
by a Teacher I Trusted*

AMBER GREGORY

© 2022, Amber Gregory.

All rights reserved. This book or any portion thereof may not be reproduced or used in any manner whatsoever without the express written permission of the publisher except for the use of brief quotations in a book review.

ANAMCHARA BOOKS
www.anamcharabooks.com

Paperback ISBN: 978-1-62524-840-4
eBook ISBN: 978-1-62524-841-1

Song on pages 145–146 © Theresa Lee Whiting. Used with permission.

The content of this book is for informational purposes only and is not intended to diagnose, treat, cure, or prevent any psychological condition. This book is not intended as a substitute for consultation with a licensed therapist. Please consult with your own physician or therapist regarding the suggestions and recommendations made in this book.

This book is dedicated to

each and every little sweetheart out there.

With love,

Amber

Contents

Introduction 9

1. The Beginning 13
2. A God of Love 17
3. Fire! 23
4. A Mixed Bag 31
5. The Sheep 37
6. The Wolf 42
7. Playing Games 52
8. That Fishy Smell 59
9. Birthday Sex 64
10. The Breakup 68
11. Soul Mates Again 74
12. Coping with Trauma 79
13. Victimization 87
14. Processing and Healing 92

15. Forgiving Yourself 102

16. Boundaries...105

17. Another Dream...................................... 112

    Afterword 127

    Exercises..129

    Definitions...139

    Further Reading 144

    New Life..145

Introduction

A few years ago I had an interesting dream. In the dream, I was feeling a little sad and alone, and I asked God to please bring into my life my soul mate. God chuckled and showed me my life as though it were a roller coaster ride, with all the ups and downs. I was enjoying the thrill of each twist and turn, each hill and tunnel, and I noticed God right there with me, sometimes very closely attached to me, sometimes way above me while I rode on alone.

I said, "See, God, this ride is great, but it would be even better if I wasn't ever alone. I would really love for You to bring my soul mate into my life." This being a lucid dream that I was dreaming, I threw in an image of my boyfriend riding next to me. I was hoping his connection to me would become that kind of close relationship I had always longed for.

But then God laughed out loud and said, "I am your Soul Mate." The image of my boyfriend disappeared, and now I saw that God was attached closely to me on the ride.

I looked at God incredulously, unable to believe the words I was hearing.

"Who else could be your soul mate, Amber?" God said. "I am the only Being connected to your soul."

At that point in the dream, I saw an image of my belly button. Maybe, I thought, it was actually the navel of my soul, the point where I still draw life from God.

"That's right," God said. "Every person is connected to Me in this way." God explained to me that the minute, no the moment, that a baby is placed under a mother's heart, that child's soul is connected to God; they are soul mates for the individual's entire life, until death and even beyond.

Still, I was reluctant to believe this. I leaned away from God, and my mind pulled up another image of my boyfriend. I wanted him to be on my roller coaster ride with me. My mind turned then to an image of my mother and my children, and my strong connections to them. These connections are the ones I feel so deep, the deepest, and yet still, I was longing for an even deeper connection. I wanted a soul-mate kind of connection.

God smiled, and I felt warmed right down to my toes. "*I am your Soul Mate.*" The tone of God's voice underlined each word.

I thought about it. I decided to try the idea on for size. As I sat with it, I started to believe it. God laughed quietly as my understanding took hold.

Can I just say, I love that I made God laugh? That's one of my favorite pieces of the dream. I love that God shared this understanding with me.

I came away from the dream with a new and deeper love for God. I continue to talk with God. That may sound crazy to some people, but let me assure you, I don't actually *hear* a voice. Instead, God is a constant sense of presence in my head. I *feel* God's intention. I sense when God smiles or laughs or wants me to question further. I always feel completely at home and safe when God speaks to me.

Anyway, after the dream, I decided to take a new look at my life, starting back from the beginning and trying to see whether my Divine Soul Mate had actually been with me through it all. And in the light of this new concept, I saw my life differently.

I tend to have a happy-go-lucky outlook on my life, but I've realized recently that this has been a coping skill I learned very young. My life story has actually had many harsh realities. Minimizing and rationalizing and dissociating have been my coping mechanisms for most of my life. "Things will work out in the long run," I've always told myself. Even when it came to truly awful things, I would still say, "Bad things are a blessing in disguise."

So as I wrote my Soul-Mate story, I faced for the first time that some things that had happened to me when I was a child were truly awful. Still, I intended my story to be about hope, not sorrow. I was discouraged when friends and even an editor read what I had written and responded with horror and pity. That wasn't at all what I was looking for.

What I wanted to convey was the transformation of looking back at my life in a new way. I wanted others who might find themselves in similar circumstances to experience the sense of possibilities and hope that I had discovered. I realize that not everyone deals with horrible events with denial and dissociation; some people carry a heavy load of resentment and bitterness and hurt. I hoped my story would allow them to transform their feelings as well.

So I found a new editor, and I went ahead and wrote the true story of what happened to me when I was young. As I wrote, I realized my beliefs about what had happened were changing— and as my beliefs changed, so did my feelings. I understood that through even the worst moments, God had been there, attached to me. God had been my Soul Mate through it all.

One

The Beginning

Babies grow up in many different ways in many different families. Despite everything that happened to me, overall I grew up feeling very blessed. Or is that my denial talking again? Maybe, but as I look back at my life with the belief that God has always been my Soul Mate, I can see now how God has always been on my side, rooting for me. God has nudged me in the right direction and introduced helpful strangers into my life. And God gave me a wild imagination to carry me away from pain and disappointments.

My mother had two children from her first marriage and then one other child and me from her second. I was born six years after my sister; you might think I was an "oops," but my mom had told my dad that if he wanted a boy, I was the last chance. They even had a boy's name ready for me—Scott. Oh well, they got me! My dad was so disappointed that for my first year of life, he insisted on calling me Scott. Luckily, I was mild-tempered and considered an easy baby.

My mother worked a lot and enjoyed it. She was a loving mother, but sometimes it seemed her work came first, ahead of her children. And maybe she preferred to stick her head in the sand about some things. Mostly, though, she was very good-natured, very creative, and always included people and made room for one more.

My father was a loving father, but he also had some shortcomings. He was often between jobs, drank too much, yelled too much, and liked to argue. To his credit, he was a very intelligent man, had a passion for recycling and environmental care, and was an avid reader of books. He also loved to sing and had a pleasing baritone voice. He sang in the chorus with the local opera for a while—and as I was growing up, he always sang in the car. My favorite car songs were sing-along ones like "The Harlem Goat," where he would sing the first line, then I would sing the same line, repeating back and forth until a comical ending.

That particular song is about a naughty goat who eats his owner's red shirts "right off" the clothesline. His owner ties him to the railroad track, where soon a train is coming. The poor goat "coughs up" the red shirts to flag the train. "But the buttons got stuck . . . in *the middle of* his throat" (here you sing the words "middle of" as crazy as you can make your voice sound)—and that is the end of the Harlem Goat, "that poor old goat."

My dad and I also enjoyed singing many songs that were sung in a round, which took me some time to master. But my favorite songs were the ones he sang alone, like "Danny Boy" and "Old Shep." My dad had a melancholy side and he would often shed a tear over sad songs.

We moved around a lot. I know how old I was by what our address was at the time; for example, when we lived at 908 Birdsall Avenue, I was two years old.

That was also the year I disappeared for an entire day without anyone noticing until my mother came home from work. I had gotten on the back of a neighborhood kid's bicycle, and we went to his house, where we played all day. When my mother got home from work and noticed I was nowhere to be found, she was in a panic. She called the police, and eventually, I was located.

That time, it was my father's absent-mindedness that was to blame, but my mother could be equally oblivious of my presence. When I was three, my family accidentally left me at a fruit stand in Pennsylvania. When they finally came back for me, I was sitting behind the counter being watched by the owner.

I have repeatedly asked my mother how she could have forgotten me there. She responds by saying, "Oh, you know how it is, Amber. When you have older kids around, you just assume one of the older ones is taking care of the younger one." As a mother now myself, I have no idea what she is talking about. The time I thought I'd lost my daughter in an amusement park was a nightmare. I carried my son in my arms while I searched frantically for her. After only three minutes or so, she was located. I clutched her close and buried my tears in her dress.

So no, I don't understand how my mother could have forgotten about me as she was picking out fresh peaches and green beans. How could she have driven away without me as though I were a purse she had put down and forgotten? What if I had wandered into the road?

I'm telling you these two little stories so you'll have an idea of the kind of parenting that went on in my family. No ill intent, but a certain lackadaisical attitude. I was loved, but in some ways, I was parented by neglect. That lack of parental attention was what made possible the events that took place when I was twelve.

But first, let me tell you some more about the years that came before.

Two

A God of Love

When I was four, God really came through for me as a Soul Mate. You might say I hit the spiritual jackpot.

That year we moved into a huge rundown house on Jenkins Avenue, right across the street from a large, brick Methodist church. That church had a parsonage, where one Christie Schmidt, age five, and her brother Robbie, age seven, lived. The Schmidts invited me into their clean, calm, beautiful life, and I accepted the invitation.

I left my shoes at the door, made sure my paws were clean, and created things like "ants on a log" (celery sticks with peanut butter and raisins) and "wagon wheels" (Ritz crackers with peanut butter). The Schmidts let me sleep over; in fact, I wiggled right into their life. We kids made up plays and songs, made forts, and colored pictures. Mrs. Schmidt pinned up my pictures right along with Christie's and Robbie's. The three of us ran around the house doing who knows what until Mrs. Schmidt called us to the kitchen table for snacks served with watered-down Kool-Aid served in Dixie cups.

I have a memory of Mrs. Schmidt leaning over me to clip my sweaty hair back with a yellow plastic butterfly barrette. Her bright orangey-red mouth was smiling at me, and I was perfectly happy.

My mother said that shade of lipstick didn't seem right for a minister's wife, but other than the odd comment about Mrs. Schmidt's makeup, I am sure my mom was glad to have me out of the way. She was dedicated to her work, and she was happy to leave me in someone else's care.

The best days at the Schmidts' house were rainy days. Mrs. Schmidt would loan me Christie's old rain boots and slicker, and Christie and I would be allowed to play in the church parking lot, splashing in puddles like ducks. I had never owned rubber boots or a slicker; wearing them felt like being in a magic suit that kept me warm and dry in a rainstorm.

That's only one of the memories I treasure from that year. I can still close my eyes and see the sunlight coming through the windows in their kitchen. Their house somehow seemed several shades lighter than mine. The Schmidt house had a shine to it, and I just couldn't seem to get enough of it.

The minutia of their lives mesmerized me. For example, Reverend Schmidt jumped rope for exercise. I thought it was so fascinating to see a grown man in workout shorts and a t-shirt doing high-speed rope-skipping in his upstairs office.

I also remember that Christie's brother Robbie sometimes wet the bed. He was a few years older than me, but his parents were never angry with him about it. Mrs. Schmidt would pull the sheets from his top bunk, telling him, "There is nothing to worry about, sweetie. It happens. We will just wash the sheets." There was a smile in her voice that made it clear she meant her words, that her love for her son wasn't dented a bit by the fact that he occasionally wet the bed. I knew that if it had been me who had wet my bed, I would have died of shame. My mom's voice would have rung with disapproval that I had made more work for her to do, and my older brother and sisters would have teased me and called me a baby.

One time when I was four something happened to me in the middle of the night. I don't know what, so don't even ask, but it scared the bejeezus out of me, and I ended up with a bloody nose. I was afraid to wake anybody up, so I went into the bathroom and stood on the toilet to look in the mirror. My face and pajama top were covered in blood. I screamed and started crying, which brought my mother stumbling sleepily from her bedroom.

"What are you doing in here?" she said. "Why is your nose bleeding? What is going on, Amber?" I felt as though I had done something wrong.

She made me sit on the edge of the tub with a wet cloth held to my nose while she sent one of my siblings to get ice for the back of my neck. She got me cleaned up, and even let me sleep with her that night, but I was overwhelmed with guilt that I had woken up everyone in the family. I got the message loud and clear that I'd been a bother.

I sometimes think my mom never really wanted to have kids. Before I had my own children, when I commented to my mother about my yearning to have kids, she said, "I don't know what to tell you, Amber. You have kids, then you deal with them."

Luckily for me, I had a Soul Mate who was looking out for me all through my childhood. I hadn't really any notion of God before I met the Schmidts, and their family was a good way to start. From them, I learned that God loved me and watched over me; God wanted me to be helpful, and God wanted me to love my mother and father. "You got it, God!" I thought. "I'm your girl!"

My theology was a little confused, though. I translated the message I learned from the Schmidts into "if you believe in God,

God will keep you safe." I think many people might have this same idea when they are young. I also think it may set us up for some heartbreak at some point in our lives. I mean, let's think about that. God's not a physical presence. The Divine can't take a bullet for you. No matter how much God loves you and is present with you, you still live in a world where bad things happen. God can help you transform the meaning of those things—but God never promised to keep them from happening.

But still, I'm grateful for all that I learned during that year when I spent so much time with the Schmidts. I started going to church and Sunday school on Sundays. At my insistence, my mom got a children's Bible-story book to read at bedtime (just like Christie's). I firmly believed in a God of love.

Then Christie started kindergarten, so I had to occupy myself during the morning. When she came home, she always wanted to play "school" where she was the teacher. One of the things she "taught" me was fire safety; she'd been learning about it in kindergarten, and she was adamant I had to learn it too.

So I dragged my mom, dad, brother, and sisters into the living room and explained how to *stop, drop, and roll,* and told them that if there ever was a fire, they needed to *check a door before you open it,* and the most important thing: *get out and get to a safe spot so everyone can meet there.* I was not allowed to cross the street by myself, but for this one exception, we agreed, I would get out, cross the street, and wait in plain sight by the church.

Christie and I loved to talk about the idea of "what if." And since fire was a hot topic, we often sat behind the huge bushes bordering her front porch and in low voices said, "What if there was a fire and you couldn't get out?"

"What if your cat got left inside?"

"What if your mom got left inside?"

"What if you were trapped on the second floor—would you jump?" and so on . . .

Well, holy cow! Our house did catch fire.

Three

Fire!

According to the newspaper, the fire was started by kids playing with candles. I remember my twelve-year-old sister loved to light candles, and the fire did start in the bedroom we shared, so the newspaper probably got it right. I was in the backyard when I heard one of my uncles yelling. I looked up and saw flames bursting out my bedroom window.

I of course did what anyone well-versed in fire safety would have done. I looked both ways, crossed the street, and stood by the church at the designated spot.

But no one else came to join me.

From across the street, I could see that my family was in a complete uproar. My mother, who sewed very fine custom draperies, feared smoke and water damage to her precious fabrics, so she was frantically carrying bolts of fabric and sewing machines out onto the front lawn. My oldest sister was throwing her clothes over the balcony railing; she had paid for most of those clothes herself, and they were precious to her. My middle sister was trying to go back into the smoking house to look for her cats, while my brother was trying to stop her...

As I stood there, waiting patiently, Mrs. Schmidt came out on her porch. She immediately saw me standing in my spot by the church and came rushing over to me.

"Are you okay? Are you hurt? Why are you here?" She put her arms around me, and I burst into tears.

At about that point, when I suppose my mother had rescued all her fabric, she shrieked, "Where's Amber? Where's Amber?"

My dad's bellow echoed, "Where's Amber? Where's Amber?"

My stomach knots up whenever I remember that moment. I know now that they were afraid for me, but at the time, I felt I must have done something wrong.

As I said earlier, my dad drank too much and yelled too much, and—well, he didn't always yell in a logical way. We kids got yelled at for completely bogus things, which tends to mess with your gauge of right and wrong. So there I was, doing the right thing, waiting at the safe spot by the church, and I was immediately scared and ashamed that I'd done the wrong thing after all.

After telling my parents where I was, the Schmidts had me wait in their house. Something was different, though. I felt like I didn't belong there anymore. It was the first time I went from feeling like everyone else, almost like a member of the family, included and liked—to feeling just downright different. I couldn't put into words what had happened, and I'm still not quite sure. The change had something to do with the way Mrs. Schmidt looked at me, the way Christie clung to her mother and was quiet. Reverend Schmidt, who seldom talked to me, tried to make conversation, but I too was quiet.

I stood at the Schmidts' front window, watching my family across the street, trying to catch a glimpse of my mother. I wished I was with her instead of the Schmidts, but at age five going on six, I had suddenly realized just how messed up my whole family really was. I knew it with a deep-down awareness that made me feel sick.

Inside my mind, I ticked off the facts about my family that were abruptly so clear to me. My mom worked so much because she paid for everything in our lives. My dad didn't contribute a dime. He didn't skip rope to stay healthy like Reverend Schmidt; instead, he smoked and drank and swore like a sailor. My oldest sister kept running away; the police would find her and bring her back, and I'd gotten used to seeing police cars by our house. She stole alcohol from my parents, got high, and was downright mean to me; she was later diagnosed as having bipolar disorder. My brother stayed in his room almost all the time unless he was teasing my middle sister by threatening to kill her cats. My middle sister was, well, different. My parents fought about her constantly: what was to be done about Laura? Today people would probably say she had ADHD and was slightly on the autism spectrum.

And then there was me. I think I was an "easy" baby and an "easy" toddler and an "easy" child because I sensed that if I weren't, my mother might really have cracked up. She has told me more than once, "You know what, Amber? We are a lot alike. I think you are my only child that I ever really enjoyed." I always felt special when my mother said that. I was just like my mom, who was seemingly the most giving and caring person I knew. It's only recently that I've realized how hungry I've always been for attention from my mother.

On the day of the fire, my brother eventually came over to get me. By then, most of the fire trucks had packed up and gone. Someone had brought us a bucket of Kentucky Fried Chicken. Our dog, Timmy, wouldn't eat chicken after that day, and my parents speculated that he remembered the fire.

I remember I started to cry, and my mom asked me what was wrong. Is it just me or does that seem like a really odd thing to ask a five-year-old when the remains of her house are still smoldering? I said I was crying because my hermit crab must have died in the fire.

My dad said, "Let's go look." He led me through the downstairs, which had a lot of water damage, and up the stairs, which had a lot of smoke damage, and into the master bedroom where piles of stuff had been piled. Lo and behold, there was the tank with several pictures and brass candle holders and photo albums piled inside it. My dad took everything out—and there was the crab, fit as a fiddle. My dad put him back in his tank, added his food, and picked the whole thing up.

My dad was funny that way. Car songs and helping me find my crab, but temperamental. His discipline often didn't make sense to me. For example, once, when I was three or four years old, I snuck a box of 9-Lives cat food out of the cupboard and went behind the living room sofa, where I was quietly crunching it, pretending I was a kitten. My mom and dad came into the room and sat down because they were having a serious talk. I have no idea what they were talking about, but I was terrified I was going to get caught eating cat food, which I knew I wasn't allowed to do. Of course, I made some noise and did get caught. My dad said, "Amber, come on out and get over here." He spanked my butt, and I started crying, certain I was being punished for munching on cat food. Then he confused me by saying, "Eavesdropping is a terrible and dishonest thing to do! Now go to bed!" I went upstairs crying the whole way, still carrying the cat-food box. I went to bed wondering what in the heck, since they didn't take the cat food away from me, I had done wrong.

So yeah, my dad could be confusing.

On the day of the fire, as we were going back downstairs, I asked if I could see my bedroom. "Sure," he said.

The door was missing. The room was a giant charcoal briquette. Nothing was left, just the charred bed frame and a few barely recognizable stuffed animals. It seemed surreal, as though this must be some other little girl's room, surely not mine.

After the fire, we stayed at a dingy hotel for a few days while my parents found another place to live. The hotel was only right around the corner from the Schmidts' home, but after the day of the fire, I didn't see Christie again until junior high school. I never went back to their church. I never asked to go visit. I wanted to stay close to my mother; in fact, I didn't want to let her out of my sight. I had realized that life could be quickly uprooted. I didn't want to be left behind or forgotten before we got established in a new house. Once I had a new address, I comforted myself, I could at least find my way home.

Another odd thing happened during the hotel stay: my mom asked my dad to move out and not move into the new house with us. My father, quite upset, called a family meeting and we all had to vote on if we should kick my father out of the house. I was not quite six years old, but yep, I got a vote too. I went along with whatever my mother wanted, and we unanimously voted it would be better if he got his own place.

And so he never moved into the new house with us at 13½ Lincoln Ave. He was still around, though, and not much changed really. At the new house, most mornings he would be at the kitchen table smoking cigarettes when I got up for school. He slept at his new apartment, but not a lot changed in my parents' relationship. It was better for us, though, because now he got drunk elsewhere, and if he tried to come over when he was drunk, my mom or my sister stopped him at the porch.

In the mornings before school, my mom put a bowl of cereal out for me and did my hair while my dad talked on and on about something or other. He would give me a one-armed squeeze and I would be off. The house was close enough I walked to my new school.

Through all of this, God was still my Soul Mate. Even though I lost the connection I had formed with the Schmidts and now I never went to church, God was still with me in a pretty big way. I said my prayers every night because I really liked to. That end-of-the-day conversation with God is something I still do.

Now of course, even if God is your Soul Mate, it's not like the Divine is going to ride bikes with you or play monopoly. I was extroverted and I craved attention. So God provided for me in the form of a dog.

My constant companion between the ages of five and ten was my dog Timmy. Man, I loved the heck out of that dog! If he hadn't been such a willing playmate, I might have gotten into a lot of trouble. He cheerfully endured getting dressed up so I could show him off by walking him on a leash around our neighborhood. He slept on my bed and made me not as afraid of the dark. He let me boss him around endlessly, playing school, where I was always the teacher and he was always the student.

That one-arm hug in the morning was about all I got from my father during those years. My mom tucked me in bed at night, but in between, from the time I came home from school until bedtime, I was pretty much on my own. My siblings were all teenagers and not interested in spending much time with me—but that was okay, I had a forty-pound, good-natured beagle-mutt. My ambassador from God—Timmy, the mixed-breed beagle. Thanks, God.

See what I mean? My Soul Mate came through for me again.

That didn't stop in the years that lay ahead—but life did start to get more complicated.

Four

A Mixed Bag

I have to admit—my childhood upbringing was pretty much a mixed bag. The older I get and the more counseling I have, the more I can see that my family left some pretty big holes in my life. But then again, in their defense, they really did do the best they could with the tools they had, considering their own beginnings. You can only teach what you know.

Take my mother. She really believes people are good, and she absolutely never gossips. She is so optimistic, and she will bend over backward to make something for others. One Christmas when we had no money, she made me a sleeping bag with a cat-face pillow attached. (This was way, way before there was one you could buy at a Walmart.)

On the other hand, she let my sister marry a much older man when Laura was only eighteen years old. The night before the wedding, Laura was hysterically sobbing that she wasn't ready and she couldn't get married. My heart nearly broke hearing her cry, but my mother merely said, "You have to, Laura. We have all these people coming from out of town. What would we tell everyone?"

Who cares? I thought. My idealistic twelve-year-old self was freaking out. I thought, *Don't make her do it, Mom! Don't make her do it!* I also assumed my sister was a virgin, and I couldn't understand why my mother would force her to have sex with this older man. At the time, I was still pretty naïve when it came to sex.

My best friend during fourth, fifth, and sixth grades was a Catholic girl named Michaela. She was appalled that I didn't know the "Our Father," and she made me learn it ASAP. (A good thing to know; thanks, Michaela.) I went to mass with Michaela and her family sometimes, and I attended a kids' Bible study on Wednesday nights. Through all that, I got another glimpse of how God is present. It also gave me some pretty puritanical views when it came to sex. Although I am sure everyone involved thought they were teaching me good values to live by, it came back to bite me later.

Michaela's mother and father were divorced, which was obviously a touchy subject with her mother. Her father had left her for a much younger woman, and according to rumor, they liked to walk around their house naked. Michaela's mother insisted he would "burn in hell" for his sins. (I thought she meant the walking around their house naked bit, not the divorcing part, but I wasn't quite sure, and I had the good manners not to ask).

Anyway, what with one thing and another, my understanding of sex was pretty limited. Dave, the older man my sister was supposed to marry, had been living with us and sharing a bedroom with my sister for at least six months or so. Once, my sister caught me looking through the keyhole of her bedroom and sat me down to ask what I had seen. Honestly, she had a bookshelf in the way, and I said I hadn't seen anything but the bookshelf. She was skeptical.

Dave said to me, "I think Laura is concerned you saw her smoking."

"Smoking!" I gasped. "I didn't know you smoked. Does Mom know? How could you? It's so dirty! You should stop!" On and on I went.

"Well," my sister said, "now that you know the secret, you will probably see me smoking in the house, but I'll try to keep it in my room or on the porch." So I never did figure out that she and Dave were sleeping together.

The eve of the wedding, I ended up going to sleep very late, my sister still crying huge wracking sobs and my mom trying to comfort her while insisting she had to go through with the wedding.

And she did. The out-of-town guests were not disappointed, and my mother was satisfied.

It turned out, though, that Dave had a closet drinking problem. My sister left him after six months, moved back in with my mom and me, dropped into the worst depression she ever had up to that point, and for three months wouldn't leave her room except to go to the bathroom. My mom seemed to think I could do something about it. "Go talk to your sister," she would say.

I tried. I failed. And by now, I had my own problems.

But before I go there, let me tell you one other highlight of my life. When I was nine, I started dance lessons.

What can I say about starting dance lessons? My first lesson I cried, because I was the sensitive kid that cried the first time I did anything away from my mom. My dance teacher was great, though. She pulled me out of my shell in five minutes—and that was all she wrote. From then on, dancing was my bliss.

I was in competition classes after the first year, doing solos, duos, trios, small group, technique, and before too long, I ended up in a senior competition class. My wonderful mother who really couldn't afford the lessons, much less twenty to twenty-five costumes per dance season, competition fees, hotel, and travel expenses, somehow managed it. See what I mean about her? She sewed my costumes and took on costumes for other students whose mothers didn't sew. She might have fallen short on time and attention, but she did the best she could for me

So let me take a moment to put in a plug for Mom. She grew up in a family that was always on public assistance. There were twelve kids in all, with my mom in the middle of the older group. They often had only potatoes or oatmeal to eat. Her own mother, my grandmother, didn't care much for girls, and when my mom was seven or eight years old, my grandmother moved out, taking only the boys with her. All the girls stayed with their father, who was an alcoholic with raging mood swings. Since bipolar disorder runs in our family, my guess is that he was undiagnosed and used alcohol to manage his symptoms. As my mom was in the older group of children, she was expected to watch the younger ones. Then when she was sixteen, she took a job as a mother's helper forty miles away from her dad. She tells the story that her stepmother played a part in her sticking to her plan to get away from her family when the woman said, "Oh don't worry, you can't make it on your own. You'll be back within the month." To spite her, my mom never went back, although she admits she was so homesick she cried almost every night. She lived with the family who hired her, finished high school in the new town, and was that family's "mother's helper" for two years. Later, as an adult, she raised four kids with no help from public assistance. She started her own business, was very successful, and still runs it after fifty years. I think she always wanted more for her children and maybe thought she wasn't the best person to teach it. But she always figured out a way to make things happen. So despite everything, my mom was also a way that God my Soul Mate was present in my life. Life's a mixed bag like that.

So geez, do I thank God for the dancing talent? For the awesome teacher who loved me and encouraged me? For the awesome mother who loved me and enabled my dance lessons? Sure, I do. But like I just said, life's a mixed bag.

God was my Soul Mate, always present in my life. But so were some other things. And they were about to mess me up pretty badly.

Five

The Sheep

When I was twelve, I wrote a story titled "The Sheep Who Was a Magnificent Dancer and Had a Secret." It went something like this:

> *There was once a dance studio that made girls into beautiful, talented dancers. The best dancers were called the "Show-Stoppers." There were twelve of them. When they danced everyone watched them and they won many awards.*
>
> *All the girls were friends. All the girls tried hard. But this story is about one dancer named Ayla.*
>
> *Ayla couldn't explain the joy she felt when she heard the music in her dance class. She couldn't explain the*

thrill she felt when she leapt through the air; she couldn't describe the head-spinning feeling she got when pirouetting on one leg then the other. She went to bed most nights exhausted and peaceful, thanking God so much for her life until she just drifted off.

One day a sheep joined their group. He was also beautiful, but in a different way from the girls. He was an unusual and magnificent dancer! Better than all the girls. He could leap higher and spin longer. He had a sheepish smile and sparkly blue eyes. All the girls wanted to be his friend. He made their group better because he was different and really talented. When he danced, you just couldn't take your eyes off him. The group started winning better awards and competing at better competitions after he joined.

The Sheep talked nicely to all the girl dancers and started asking Ayla to be his partner when doing practice steps across the floor. At first, it just seemed like he was being nice, but then the Sheep continued to single out Ayla, and they were partners every time. Ayla was flattered. After a short while, the Sheep put a casual arm around Ayla and steered her away from the other girls where he could have a private conversation with her. Ayla felt a thrill, like she'd just leaped as high as she could!

A little more time went on, and then, as the Sheep and Ayla were sitting next to each other waiting for their turn to dance, the Sheep whispered to her, "Can I tell you a secret?"

Ayla's tummy did a flip-flop. "Yes!" she whispered back.

"I think I'm falling in love with you," he said, and he blinked his sparkly blue eyes slowly.

For a second, though, she thought he had yellow gleaming eyes—but then the sparkly eyes were back. Ayla's heart started racing. What had those yellow eyes meant? She couldn't have seen that right. In any case, when he smiled his sheepish smile that crinkled his blue eyes so charmingly, she soon forgot that glimpse of yellow eyes. She smiled right back, already half in love with him.

More time went on, and Ayla and the Sheep passed each other secret notes. They were always each other's partners, and now, instead of telling God about how happy dancing made her, Ayla went to bed every night telling God how excited the Sheep made her, and how thrilling the feeling of his friendship was. She wanted to touch him and see how soft he was. Her head was filled with how beautifully he leaped through the air and turned just perfectly, and she prayed that he always wanted to be her special friend. She told God she would do anything to keep that special exclusive friendship.

As the end of the dance year came around, the "Show-Stoppers" were in charge of painting the scenery for the recital. All the girls and the Sheep were at the studio painting. They were running out of paint so the Sheep offered to go buy some. He asked Ayla if she wanted to ride along. Of course she did!

They were out the door heading to his car when he said, "Uh-oh. I left something upstairs." And then he added, with that smile that crinkled his blue eyes, "Come with me."

Ayla followed him up a dark back stairwell and at the top, he shoved her roughly into a room with a mattress. Instead of her friend the Sheep, suddenly a yellow-eyed wolf was holding her down with his teeth tangled in her hair. He growled in her ear, "Shut up! Do you want everyone to know what we are doing?"

"NO!" Ayla squeaked. But she meant, "No, stop! You're hurting me!"

That is how the Wolf came into my life. Because, as I'm sure you've gathered, that story wasn't fiction. It was exactly what happened to me when I was twelve years old.

And that stinking Wolf did hurt me. He hurt me in the worst way a young, innocent girl of twelve could be hurt, and I cried and said no, and he held me down. When it was over, he hurt me even worse by turning back into the Sheep, drying my tears and then turning it all around.

He said he thought that I'd wanted what happened because I secretly passed him notes, and I followed him up the stairs.

"After all," he said, "why else would we have gone up there if you hadn't wanted what happened. And of course," he added, "everyone knows now because we were gone so long and you made so much noise, so we had better act like we are in love. If we don't, they will all just think you're a bad girl."

That was the end of my childhood.

Six

The Wolf

As an adult, I can look back and see that several things led up to the rape that were key to it having occurred.

First, it was not a straight rape, where someone attacks you and it's over. The Wolf took his time stalking me. He started easy, probably singling me out because my mother was never around the studio. Since she worked all the time, I was just dropped off and picked up. That meant the Wolf had time to cultivate a relationship with me on the sly and not get caught.

Years later, when my mother found out what had happened to me, she cried. She said she thought I was safe at the studio, and if she had known what happened, she would have done something. I believe her. If there hadn't been a wolf at my studio,

I would have been just fine. Dance was one of the best parts of my life and remained so even after the walk up those stairs.

There was also no father at home in my house; in fact, there was no one to pay much attention to me. Oh sure, I had an affectionate dog, but that relationship got blown out of the water by the attention of an older, attractive, wildly talented boy who was literally the superstar of our studio.

I had been moved into a competition group my second year of dancing when I was ten. That group was with other ten-year-olds who had been dancing their whole lives; most started dance at age three or four, so I was proud of myself. I was even more proud when I was moved into the senior competition group, the Wolf's group, when I was twelve. I was good enough and it helps keep the age average down for competitions; in other words, the Wolf's group made up of mostly fifteen- to eighteen-year-olds could compete in a younger category if there were a twelve-year-old in the class to keep the average age down, making them more likely to win.

The Wolf started teaching at the studio that year, and the dance teacher in charge asked my mom if he could teach my solo. The teacher said she thought I would benefit from private lessons, but while she herself was too busy and had a full schedule, the Wolf was a senior dancer, who had been dancing fifteen years at that point and could oversee my instruction. We paid a discounted price, which made my mother happy; we thought it was a great opportunity for me to get private lessons, especially so I could keep up with my older competition class.

Of course, looking back, I wish my mother had seen the red flags going up when an older boy was teaching a younger girl in one-on-one lessons. Seems like a recipe for trouble, doesn't it? But the Wolf was such a sweet boy, and my mother was glad to see me thrive at dancing. She knew I loved it so much and was excelling, and she was happy for me. She worked extra to pay for it, feeling the discipline and team effort would pay off in my life. And she wasn't wrong. It did. Had there been no Wolf at the studio, my life might have soared to even greater heights. Who knows?

When I started the dance year in September, nothing seemed amiss. The Wolf was openly dating one of the older girls named Stacy, and I was just happy to be included in the class; I wanted to fit in with the older girls and not be the "weak link" holding anyone back. My private lessons started a month later, in October. Again, everything seemed normal to me. I respected the Wolf the same way I respected my proper dance teacher, and I worked hard on the moves he was teaching me in private lessons, just like I was working hard in all my classes. I have it in me to stick to things, and the private lessons were paying off.

Around Christmas, things changed a little. The Wolf gave me a Christmas present. It was a tiny felt teddy bear that said "You are beary special" in a red heart. It made my heart race. As soon as I saw it, I began thinking about him as a boy rather than just respecting him as my dance teacher.

I started being careful about how I dressed. I took an interest in fashion and what the other girls were wearing. I kept my eyes on the Wolf constantly. I was delighted when he pulled me out to be his partner to demonstrate moves, or lightly touched my shoulders to direct me into place.

I was sure he had no idea I was paying so much attention to every move he made. When he talked to Stacy, I intently absorbed how she smiled or frowned at him. I did notice her frowning at me a lot, but I had done nothing; on the surface, I was certain I was just trying hard as usual to please both my dance teachers.

After Christmas, my private lessons became my favorite day of the week. The Wolf made a point of moving me into places by guiding me by my shoulders or teasing me and pulling me by my ponytail around in circles. He was like a playful cousin, I told myself. Having all that superstar charm wattage directed at me made my head spin and my tummy tingle. I giggled right on cue and couldn't have contained my joy if my life depended on it.

In February, at the end of my lesson when I usually was dismissed, he called me over to the stereo system. I obediently went over to where he was sitting on a stool that put him at eye level with me. He said he had something to tell me, and he had been wanting to say it for a long time, even though it was wrong to say it. I watched his face, curious and waiting. He reached out and gently held one of my hands; I felt sparks leaping between our fingers, and I stopped breathing. He had the sweetest look on his face when he said he knew it was wrong because he was dating Stacy, but he thought he was falling in love with me.

I was embarrassed and looked down. He took his other hand, lifted my chin, and kissed me gently and sweetly on the lips. My first kiss. It was pure magic; no princess in any fairytale had anything on me. He said I had better go, it was late and he had another class, but he would write me a note. I left floating on a cloud.

He and I started writing notes to each other, and throughout the month of March, we spent the last five minutes of each of my private lessons gently kissing and exploring each other with soft touches and caresses. By April, he had brushed his hands across my breasts on the outside of my bodysuit and guided my hands to his penis on the outside of his Lycra pants. By the end of April, we were French kissing and touching skin.

All of this had been in secret, so Stacy wouldn't find out. It never even crossed my mind to complain that he had a girlfriend. He was explaining in his notes that he wasn't very happy with her, and he was going to have to end it. But he just didn't want to be mean to anyone, and she hadn't really done anything wrong, he just started liking me . . . and that wasn't her fault. I was just so sweet and special and he couldn't help having feelings for me. I bought it all.

By May, he started writing that he was sure he was falling in love with me. One day in our group class, he bounded up to me, picked me up, and swung me around in front of everyone, including Stacy.

When Stacy left the dance room crying, he went after her. They broke up.

After that, he didn't ask me out officially, but he did start being more openly flirty with me. One time, we girls were waiting in the break room. He would have usually spent that time hanging out with Stacy in his car. Instead, he waited in the lunchroom with us, chatting and turning on the charm. He decided to "fix" my hair. As he laughed and joked while braiding my hair, I had mixed feelings. The other girls were Stacy's friends. I was much younger, but I was also thrilled he was near me and touching me in such a personal way. Up until that point, only my mother or sister had brushed and braided my hair. He ended by tickling my nose with the end of the braid. I fell in love.

In June, when I followed him up the back stairwell, I didn't expect we would go "all the way," but I was pretty excited that we would be doing some kissing and touching and maybe even make third base. The force and roughness and how fast and pressured it all was scared me. And it *hurt*.

When I cried, he said, "But I thought you loved me. I love you, and I thought you wanted to be my girlfriend. I thought we would get married someday. I know you said no, but your eyes said yes."

And I did love him, and I did want to be his girlfriend. I did want to be married someday. He had just said he loved me, and that made my heart glow—but my body was hurting. I was so mixed up and embarrassed. I knew all the older girls were right downstairs, and the last thing he said was, "Well, you had better decide to be my girlfriend because with all the noise you were making everyone knows what we were doing up here. You don't want them thinking you are just a bad girl, do you?"

And of course I didn't want that. I had spent the entire year trying to prove I had been a good enough dancer to even be in their group. I never felt like I truly belonged, but in those minutes after he raped me, I felt the chasm of "them" and "me" open up to infinity. I knew I didn't belong anywhere or with anyone. Not really.

I had suddenly become someone I no longer recognized. I longed to go back to that moment before we went up the stairs together. But I couldn't.

He hurt me, and it hurt for a long time, and he hurt me worse by turning it all around and making me believe it was my fault. It crushed me. I felt I could only blame myself. The idea that it might not have been my fault after all literally took years, decades, for me to come to terms with.

If I felt like "God's girl" from age four to age twelve, I felt like I wasn't fit to be the dirt beneath God's feet after my walk up the stairs with the Wolf.

This was a defining event for me, as much as meeting the Schmidts had been, but where the one had been positive, this was deeply, darkly negative. It changed me. It changed how I thought of God and how I thought of other people. Up until then, I thought I had been living a "blessed" life. I assumed that all I had to do was hold up my end of the bargain, be a "good girl," "obey the rules," and God would bless me in return with love and happiness. I felt loved and happy and safe; I had friends, and I felt I belonged somewhere in the world. I had been told by my mom that most people were "good" and you could trust them. So I did.

After this, I was probably in a state of shock, because I had been hurt. Physically hurt, by my love, my friend, my confidant—and then he said I was going to be seen as a "bad girl," which shocked me further. How did my world shift so utterly in just a short span of time and space? How could this have happened to me, the "good girl"? The one who knew to get to safety while the house burned down, the one whom Mom enjoyed the most of all her kids because I made it easy for her, the one who got put in the competition dance classes after one year and senior competition class after three years. The one who was in all the accelerated classes at school and was sure to be the first one in our family to go to college someday. The "good girl," who was clean and didn't swear and got along so well with her mother. Who played pinochle with our extended family on card night, whom everyone loved.

Now I was being told I was going to be just a "bad girl" unless I was the Wolf's girlfriend. We only went "all the way " because he thought *I* wanted to, so it was all my fault. My mind struggled to grasp that I had become a "bad girl" and there would be no going back.

This was the first time in my life a mistake was made—and there was nothing that I could do to undo this mistake. It was irrevocable. My virginity lost, so young and before marriage.

My status as a human being had fallen to the lowest of the low in my mind.

I wish I could say I was raped once by the Wolf, and then he lost interest in me—but that is not what happened. I believed the only thing I could do to redeem the situation was to commit myself for life to the Wolf.

Seven

Playing Games

My thirteenth birthday came around, and all the kids from school and the dance studio were invited, including the Wolf. It was a fun party on the first day of summer, with a cookout and water balloons and hose fights. The Wolf publicly gave me a stuffed animal and a card. The card had a cartoon lion on the front and said: "It's hard to be humble, when you are great."

He'd added his signature and a note: "Keep this because I'm going to be famous someday, and it will be worth something."

I was a little disappointed. I had expected something more romantic or at least something saying I was "sweet" or "special."

But the Wolf stayed to the very end of the party, and he got in good with my mom by helping clean up. Then he asked her if he could take me out for ice cream. I got butterflies in my stomach in a good way. Instead of going for ice cream, though, he said he had a special present for me, but he had left it at his house. His parents weren't home, and we ended up in their rec room. There, he gave me a gold Mizpah necklace that was engraved with the words: "May the Lord watch over thee while we are separated one from another." He wore one half and I wore the other.

He told me how much he loved me and started to kiss and touch me very roughly. I confess, I sort of liked it, but I was also afraid we would end up having sex again. This would be the second time and I still remembered the pain and humiliation from the first time. I tried to say no. But once again he refused to listen.

"Wolf?" I pleaded. "I love you too, but I'm scared. Can we slow down?"

He looked at me with tragic, considerate eyes. "Oh you poor baby, did it really hurt last time?"

"Well . . . yes," I answered, heaving a big sigh of relief. He didn't understand how rough he had been, I was thinking. Boys really couldn't help themselves, like my mother had told me. He was a lovable guy, and the whole thing had been a terrible mistake.

But then he said, "Well, was it a good hurt or a bad hurt? Because I was planning on having some fun this summer."

Uh-oh. If I said it was a bad hurt, he might dump me—and I had been thinking if we got married, I could make good with God. So I lied and said, "I guess if I think about it, it was a good hurt." I ducked my head, but not before I saw that he was grinning from ear to ear. He pressed against me, and I could feel how excited he was.

"We just need to do it a few more times," he said. "Then it will stop hurting so much."

So of course we had sex again. And it was my fault, because I hadn't said no.

But no. Looking back I have to forgive my thirteen-year-old self. It wasn't her fault. Anyone with morals would have seen the reluctance on my face and in my body. As he was kissing me, I was pushing away from him, and he practically had to pry my legs apart. When he touched me, he found I was completely dry, so he spit on me to lubricate me. I was very aware that he had literally spit on what I had considered my most sacred place. For some reason, this was worse than anything else. I dissociated from the actual sex act and focused only on that one nauseating, humiliating thing: *he spit on me!*

I was not only horribly humiliated; it also hurt. The next day, I couldn't wear shorts because there were bruises on my inner thighs. No, I wasn't having a good time, not that night and not the rest of the summer.

But after that, he proclaimed to the world that we were a couple. We openly held hands and occasionally kissed in front of the other girls at the studio.

Why did no adult say anything about an older boy dating someone who was barely thirteen? The Wolf often dated and then broke up with girls in the class, so I assume the studio owner, my beloved dance teacher, didn't see this as much more than another fling. She also happened to be the Wolf's mother, and he was for sure the apple of her eye. She was so proud of him and how talented he was. He wanted to become a dance teacher and choreographer, following in her footsteps. I think he really could do no wrong in her eyes. So he stayed on her good side, and all the studio mothers loved him as well. He seemed mature for his age, a very sweet and very kind sensitive soul.

As we were an official couple now, he assumed we would have sex whenever he wanted. I didn't stop him, but I don't think I would call it consent. Legally, of course, a thirteen-year-old cannot give consent; it's considered sexual abuse by any court. But I didn't know that then. I was in a situation I had no idea how to handle, and there was no adult to help me.

So we had sex in the room above the dance studio, where I was careful to be as quiet as a mouse while I lay under him trying not to cry. We also had sex in the back of his car; we parked where he thought it would be romantic to be under the stars.

We talked often about how what we were doing wasn't really wrong because we loved each other so much—and we would be married someday. And yet I still couldn't keep myself from crying.

"Why are you crying?" he always asked, but I had no answer.

Really, I was crying because the stress of the situation was making me crack. I had been begging God to forgive me for having sex before marriage and bargaining that I would promise to marry the Wolf if God would forgive me—but I didn't want to be touched anymore, much less climbed on with my legs spread apart for the Wolf. It hurt every time. Every time, I wanted to disappear.

I was having to have sex now because in my thirteen-year-old mixed-up logic I was thinking, "If the Wolf is going to marry me and make this all right in God's eyes, then I had better please the Wolf." But I wanted to die every time he even touched me. I couldn't imagine how I would marry and be forever with a Wolf I couldn't stand to have touch me.

So when he asked me why I was crying, I finally lied and said, "I am just so happy to know that you love me so much."

He brushed my tears away and kissed me gently. "You're the sweetest girl I've ever known," he told me.

That summer when we went to dance competitions, we had sex in hotel rooms. Sometimes, we would be sneaking around, with him elated by this fun game and me laughing and playing along like he was my favorite flavor of ice cream and I just couldn't get enough—but the whole time, I was playing my own game of maneuvering ways to avoid him.

One weekend I spent the night at a girl's house I barely knew because I didn't want to go home. I knew If I were at home, the Wolf would be calling and wanting to make plans with me. I couldn't say no to him, because I didn't want him to get mad at me—so I acted like this newfound friend was a total riot and begged to stay at her house another night. Oh, the act I had going! That entire summer was such a mess.

I was terrified my mother would find out I was having sex. She knew I was dating the Wolf, and why she let me date an older boy is a mystery to me . . . but oh, wait, my sister had just married a man much older than her. I guess my mom just didn't think the age difference was wrong or weird.

I was also petrified I was going to get pregnant—and then the whole world would know what was really going on. I called Planned Parenthood and made an appointment to get birth control pills. I told my mom I was going to a friend's house, but really I rode a bus for the first time to a nearby city and followed the directions to the clinic. I checked in, answered the questionnaire, had my first pelvic exam, and answered honestly that I was "sexually active," which made my shame and dirty feelings so real I started crying. I couldn't get the tears to stop.

When the doctor and nurses got me through the exam and gave me the pills and instructions, it was over, but I was still crying, tears rolling endlessly out of my eyes. They took me to a back hallway, and a woman sat with me while I tried to pull myself together. Eventually, I managed to stop crying. I have no idea what that woman thought, but I got out of there with my pills in a brown paper bag and an appointment card for a follow-up appointment.

So over the course of the summer, I was trying to both be in love with the Wolf and dodge him. I didn't have much experience with lies, and all this deception took a toll. Just when my looks seemed critically important (after all, the Wolf *had* to marry me if I were going to make good with God), my face broke out in red, ugly pimples. I desperately needed to be pretty—but there was nothing I could do to make those pimples go away.

I also started arguing with my mother, taking my stress out on her. I called her stupid. I said she was fat and ugly, and I asked why I had to get stuck with her poor genes and not get my father's lean figure and better looks. I slammed doors. I yelled and cried. My family laughed it off and said, "Oh, Amber has finally hit puberty."

And then I started to smell like a fish.

Eight

That Fishy Smell

Everyone who came near me could smell me. I wanted to die of embarrassment. I took baths and showers and soaped and soaked, but I couldn't get the smell to stop. I started wearing Love's Baby Soft perfume and lots of makeup.

"Oh great," I would say to myself. "My face looks like a pizza pie and I stink like rotting fish. The Wolf will never marry me now. I'll never be anything more than damaged goods."

I was pretty sure the rotting-fish smell was because of the sex. Maybe I had an infection. There was no one I could ask. But the Wolf didn't seem to mind the odor. He just cracked the window of his car when he picked me up for a date.

I was still convinced I loved him; I just didn't like being with him. And I desperately needed him to love me. But I was starting to worry.

You might think the Wolf would have been over the moon to finally be able to show all of his unrequited love for me—but a funny thing happened after the initial rape. He started treating me less nicely. He wasn't sweet to me in public anymore. He no longer passed me notes or braided my hair. He didn't spin me around by my ponytail, laughing with me.

Instead, he started passing notes on the sly with another girl. Often, he abandoned me in public and hung out with the older girls, making fun of my acne in a voice that was loud enough for me to hear. My face burned with shame and embarrassment.

In private, though, he still turned on the charm. He talked often about how we were "making love," not "having sex." Nothing we did was wrong, he said, because we would be married someday.

By the middle of July, I was feeling very conflicted. Sometimes, I wanted him to dump me for the other girl; then she could be the one to be spit on. Other times, I yearned for him to love only me, and I would turn myself inside out trying to please him. I would try to flirt and get playful sexually. I acted as though I were burning with desire for him—and all the while, I'd also be dodging his phone calls. I think I cried every day that summer.

He did love me, I told myself. That's why we were having sex. I was too young to understand what was going on. And then he introduced me to new kinds of sex, and I was revolted. Oral sex made me want to throw up.

My life was a pendulum, swinging from one extreme to another. Each end of the pendulum's swing brought more tears.

He is falling in love with a new girl: *tears.*

I have done something so wrong, no one will want me now, and God won't let me go to heaven if I don't marry him: *tears.*

What if I get pregnant? *Tears.*

Even worse kinds of sex made me feel embarrassed and humiliated to my core: *tears*

I am the worst daughter ever when I speak to my mother: *tears.*

I am so ugly: *tears.*

The Wolf commented that I was putting on weight: *tears.*

What if he stops loving me? *More tears.*

During a sleepover, my best friend found the story I'd written about the rape, the one about the Sheep that turned into the Wolf. She wanted to talk about it; she wanted to tell my mother. I tried to shake her off by saying the story was about another girl at the studio. I finally ended up not calling her for months. Estranged from my best friend on top of everything else, all I could do was cry some more.

Later that summer, I bombed at competitions doing my solos, which were choreographed by the Wolf. It was his first year of teaching, and my performance was important to him, but I didn't even get an honorable mention. He was so disappointed he punished me by only having quickies with me in the hotel room; he barely looked at me or talked to me the entire weekend. I cried even more.

In fact, one quickie was in a room with other people. He led me over to a dark corner and put me on the floor. I wiggled away, trying to say no. I could hear one of the mothers talking and joking as she pulled her daughter's hair into a tight bun. The Wolf put his hand over my mouth and stared me in the eye while he pulled my shorts and underwear aside enough to push himself into me. He spit on his other hand to lubricate me, then held me down. I looked into his eyes with his hand over my mouth and didn't make a sound. I was praying no one would come over to that part of the room— and that he would be the quickest ever. That time, there was no time for tears

By August, I had so little self-confidence left that I didn't believe I could even walk into a room right. I felt like a big, ugly, fishy, pimply, clumsy, stupid girl. I would say something and immediately contradict it with, "Oh, I'm so stupid. I don't know why I said that."

The Wolf made fish jokes about my odor. During summer lessons, the studio was boiling hot—and I was stinking up the joint. That fishy smell just wouldn't go away.

And I knew I couldn't go on like this much longer.

Nine

Birthday Sex

The Wolf's birthday was in August. That was the night, I stopped praying to God. It was clear to me I was on my own.

We were in the room over the studio, where the oral sex had gone on for a long time, with me beneath him feeling choked and hot. Then came the vaginal sex, which I endured. But what broke me that night was the snuggling that came after. He spooned with me, whispering sweet things into my hair, and I couldn't stop the tears that came. The contrast between what he was saying and what had come before was just too great.

If this is what love was between a man and a women, I thought, I would give up love forever. Something shifted inside of me. I stopped talking to God then and there. I would be damaged goods and go unloved my whole life, but I would not spend my life like this any longer.

He fell asleep, and I lay quietly, sweating, the tears rolling down my cheeks, not moving a muscle or making a sound so I didn't wake him. I had to be home by midnight, and I did not want any time left for more sex. At 11:30, I woke him up and said he had to take me home so I wouldn't miss my curfew. He decided we had time for a "quickie"—it was, he reminded me, his birthday after all. He saved time by not spitting on me and went right to penetration. It hurt a lot, but it was quick: only three or four strokes, and he was done. I lay crushed under him, and then suddenly he sprang up. "Get up!" he hissed. "Get dressed! Let's go! We're going to be late!"

I dressed in the dark and crept down the stairs after him and into his car. When he immediately cracked the window, I tried not to notice, but I knew it was my smell that made him need the fresh air. I flipped down the visor mirror to fix my makeup.

I was unrecognizable.

My hair was plastered against my head every which way, and my eyes and cheeks were blurred with mascara. The lip gloss on my mouth had been kissed away, and my lips looked puffy and red. All that makeup I'd started wearing now looked like it had been applied by a drunken clown.

Who was this Amber?

I wanted to cry again. Instead, I finger-combed my hair into a bun and fixed it with a hair tie I had in my purse. There, that was a little better. I pulled a wipe out of my purse and scrubbed away the left-over makeup. Having a pizza face, I decided, was much better than being covered with the mess I saw in the mirror. I added lip gloss and smiled at myself in the mirror. I could recognize myself again.

"I hope I'm not late," I said in a light tone. I gave him a sweet smile that even crinkled my eyes.

My mom wasn't really that strict about curfew, so I wasn't particularly worried. "I'll get you there on time, baby," he said and stepped on the gas.

"I hope you had a *great* birthday," I chirped, still smiling.

"The best, baby." He didn't even give me a sideways glance.

When he pulled up in front of my house, I gave him a quick kiss and dashed inside.

I knocked on my mom's bedroom door and opened it. "Mom, I'm home."

"What time is it?" she mumbled.

"Midnight," I said.

"Okay, honey. Good night. I love you."

"Love you, Mom. Good night"

I headed straight for the bathroom, where I turned on the hot water to fill the tub. I took another look in the mirror. Wow. Thank God no one was awake to see me come in. ("No," I reminded myself, "you're not talking to God anymore.") Even with the quick bun and no makeup, I was a terrible sight. My entire face was puffed up and blotchy, and in the dark, I had put my shirt on inside out.

I stripped down and got in the tub. I put my underwear in with me to scrub out the marks of sex and blood, along with the smell . . . and finally, I truly cried, huge heaving sobs. No one heard me, and I wanted it that way. I was on my own now, I knew, and I was going to have to get myself out of this mess without anyone knowing what had happened. There was no one I could turn to for help.

Jen

The Breakup

I broke up with the Wolf a week later. When I gave him back his necklace, he actually cried big tears.

"What did I do wrong?" he begged. "Things were so perfect between us. Remember, we were going to be married someday?" Then he gave me a sly look and said, "If you don't marry me, what will God think?"

As far as I was concerned, God could go hang. I was going to take charge of things for a while.

Maybe the Wolf had truly fooled himself into believing that what we had was love. Or maybe he just liked manipulating me.

"Well, you are just too old for me," I said in a soothing voice. "I am not ready for such a serious relationship. But I am so sorry I hurt you. I hope we can still be friends."

After everything that had happened, I was trying to comfort him. I didn't change my mind about breaking up, but I did feel guilty. In fact, I felt horrible. Despite all he had done to me, I still believed I was to blame.

One of my coping skills is to be so bright and cheery and chatty that no one in the world can possibly believe there is anything wrong with me. Prior to all this, I hadn't had much reason to deceive people, but now the Actress Amber was born. I shined it on so bright that even I didn't think things were so bad.

It never occurred to me that I'd been the victim of rape until a decade later when a counselor told me the facts. I was dumbfounded.

"No," I protested. "I asked for it. I passed him notes. I said I loved him. I followed him up those stairs."

My mother had always told me that when it came to sex, boys couldn't help themselves. "It is up to you, Amber," she said, "to not ever get yourself into a bad situation." But what had I done? I'd gone and got myself into a situation where the poor Sheepy-Wolf couldn't be blamed for what had happened. It was all my fault.

"I mean," I told the counselor, "he said he would marry me. But I went and dumped him. I was the one who ruined my chance of making an honorable match and redeeming myself with God. I mean, I consented after the first time, so I might as well have said yes to all of it."

I did not like the idea that I had been raped. Not raped, not sexually abused, not messed with. No, none of that. I had made a mistake, I dealt with it, and I was living with the consequences. I was not a victim. Of course, I often called myself *stupid* and an *idiot* and a *dumb ass*—but I was not a victim.

After the breakup, I told people, "I was just too young. It just didn't work out. We are just going to be friends."

He was already passing notes to Kelly, the new girl at the dance studio, so he didn't contradict this story. I continued to take classes at the studio, but I kept a wary eye on him while he stalked the next girl—and then when that ended, the next girl, and when that ended, the next girl . . .

Each time, he followed the same cycle. First, he would charm the girl with compliments and little touches. Once he had her, though, the sly cutdowns started, along with the seemingly harmless teasing of the next girl. He usually went for the younger ones, the new girls in the class.

Meanwhile, he was polite to me, but he barely noticed if I did a good job or a bad job in class. Sometimes he touched me to move me into place, but his touch was indifferent now, meaningless. It seemed like whatever that summer had meant to me, for him it was largely forgettable.

Two years later, when he was teaching a group class, he opened a Coke by the stereo system and it fizzed up, making a puddle on the floor. I don't think anyone but me even noticed, but I was still keeping an eye on him, even after so much time had gone by. He turned, then unexpectedly came over to me and put out his hand with a grin. "Amber, give me your hand"

I hesitated and took a step back. I was no longer his favorite for demonstrations, and I didn't trust him. He quickly turned to the nearest girl with the same grin. "Sally, give me your hand."

She started to move forward, but something in me still wanted to please him.

"No, I'll do it." Smiling, I took his outstretched hand.

He spun me in such a way that he grabbed up my second hand. Then with a slight twist of his hands, I found myself sitting on the floor in the puddle of spilled soda. He dragged me forward through it, mopping it up with my butt, while he and the rest of the class laughed.

I was fifteen years old but I felt like I was five. The tears pricked at the corners of my eyes, and suddenly, I felt as though

I were back beside the Methodist church, watching my house burn down, all alone. Once again, I had managed to do the wrong thing.

I tried to join in the laughter, though. What a funny joke! I didn't have another leotard in my bag, so the Coke stain stayed on my butt for the rest of the night, an ongoing humiliation.

Why had I wanted him to pick me? Why had I still sought his approval? Once again, I knew it was all my fault.

When I was about thirty, I saw him at the post office. Didn't I give him a big smile and say, "Hi, Wolf, how are you? I hope you are doing well. It's nice to see you."

What in the heck is wrong with me?

He did a number on me, that is for sure.

Later, when I confided my story to some friends, they denied that the Wolf was a rapist. Not exactly. "After all," they said, "he was just a teenager. Maybe he really thought you wanted to have sex. He gave you that necklace; he said he wanted to marry you; he cried when you broke up. Maybe it was real for him. He was young too."

So let me tell you something I found out years later. The Wolf was arrested at a hotel when he was twenty-seven years old, because he had checked in with a thirteen-year-old girl who was one of his dance students. He pled guilty to rape.

He was arrested again when he was thirty-nine years old for having non-consensual sex with a minor under age seventeen. She was one of his students, even though after the first arrest, he was not allowed to teach children. Again he pled guilty.

The Wolf was a rapist. He raped me, not just that first time but again and again. He ended my childhood, and for a time, he destroyed my relationship with God.

But that didn't last. God was still my Soul Mate.

Eleven

Soul Mates Again

I know now that God never wanted me to marry the Wolf to "make it right." That was the confused belief of a little girl. The night of the birthday sex when I told God "to go hang," I can imagine the Hosts of Heaven cheering, all the angels playing trumpets, God and everyone else pumping their fists in the air and giving each other high fives.

"Yes, Amber! Yes!" I picture them cheering. "You got it, honey!"

"This feels wrong and you feel sad," I now hear God saying to that thirteen-year-old girl, "because it *is* wrong—but you got it, girl! Now go for it. Break up with this guy and get out of this mess, you beautiful child."

Back then, though, I felt I was disappointing God. I stopped praying for several years—but God didn't "go hang," and God didn't forsake me. God stayed right with me as a perfect Soul Mate always will, there for you when you need them, rooting for you, cheering you on—and no hard feelings if you try to ignore them for a while.

And despite how I felt on the outside, God kept my bright shiny soul as bright and shiny as the day it was placed under my mother's heart for me to grow. God gave me a spark that made me uniquely "Amber," a spark that connected me first to my mother and then to all other living things. My spark had dimmed, thanks to my experience with the Wolf—but I believe God protects our souls our whole lives, keeping them perfect and shiny and uniquely ours. The spark of our personality can fade or even go out if we experience enough trauma, but underneath, that shiny soul will be as bright and beautiful as the day God gave it to us.

Boy, do I wish someone had explained to me when I was thirteen that I really wasn't alone at all. My trusted Soul Mate was right there with me, fully connected in the only way God can be. I wish I knew about the Soul-Mate connection then. I needed it. Maybe if I knew without a doubt that even though my Soul Mate wasn't going to come riding to my rescue, God had not abandoned me, I wouldn't have turned so completely to the Wolf for the connection he offered me. Being the Wolf's girlfriend took away my sense of God's presence. Instead of turning to God for my affirmation and self-worth, I was relying on a manipulative teenage boy.

I am just recently understanding that my lack of understanding of my personal loving connection to God made my abuse worse. When something confusing and traumatic happened to me, I turned to the hand that was abusing me for a connection, any connection and comfort. I'd been misguided by religious dogma that said if I was no longer a virgin, then I was tainted and undesirable. The Wolf had me convinced that the only way back to my previous state of being a "good girl" was to continue my relationship with him, thereby allowing my soul to be abused as well as my body.

I wonder how things might have been different if I had been told in Sunday school that God was my Soul Mate—always connected, always on my side, always affirming me and attached to me permanently in a way that could never be broken or divided. No matter what happened to my physical body or my emotions.

I wish my mother and father had nurtured my belief in God. I think if I had believed God was not just up there and I was down here, that my Soul Mate was ever-present, always on my side, cheering for me, delighting in me, ready and willing to be patient with my tantrums or naughtiness, still bound to me by bonds incapable of breaking, watching and willing me to grow strong and tall and true in my heart and deeds, then I think I would have valued myself more. I wouldn't have been afraid of displeasing God. Maybe I would have been more confident in myself and not manipulated by a belief that I was disappointing God in so many ways.

Why did God not ride to my rescue? Why does God allow thirteen-year-olds to be raped? Why does evil exist? I believe that is not the relationship God has with us. That is not God's promise to us. God will be with us. Our souls are protected and nothing will damage them. I also believe at the end of this life, we get to go back home to God no matter what path got us through. But in between? Well, I believe God wants us to take action in our lives. Not depend on a fairy godmother who corrects all of life's shortcomings so we are living a life of ease. Not in this life. In this life, we are here to struggle and wrestle and conquer—and shine with the knowledge *we* can do it!

We all have free will. Some of us use that will to hurt others of us. Why didn't God stop it? I know God loved me. I used to think "Funny how God showed it by letting such despicable events unfold."

I now think of God differently. I know God was with me the whole time the Wolf was stalking me and I know God was with me during the attack and I know God was with me after, although *I* pushed God away then and didn't want God to be near me. I think the Wolf bruised my body and those hurts healed, and I think he damaged me emotionally, and those wounds took many years to heal. Those hurts and the mistrust of men, I carried right into every love relationship I have ever had with a man. But the Wolf didn't touch my soul. That shiny thing is as perfect it ever was. Just as shiny as its connection to God will always keep it.

When bad things happen to us, or things don't go our way we all say "Why did God let this happen? Why didn't God do something? Why would God do this to me?" Or a variation thereof. Truth: God never ever promised to ride into your life like a knight in shining armor and get you out of a terrible situation. Just like God never rode bikes with you when you were a kid. I believe God wants us to love each other and be kind and caring, and I think we have Divine opportunities to relate to each other in positive ways. But not every person believes this or acts accordingly. Even though many children are traumatized in the same way I was, God also provided me with a way to reframe this hurt and sadness and see the trauma and my fear of God in a different way.

I want to pass this new concept on to other people, to reframe their trust in God, to believe God was and is still there for them. Always. And God will help them cope with life's traumas.

Twelve

Coping with Trauma

Going back in my memory and pulling out details from a period of time I have spent minimizing and rationalizing for decades was hard, and I cried a lot. One editor I met calls these remembrances while writing "wet pages," because you can't help but cry as you write. She says that both the tears and the writing help us cope with the traumas we've endured.

Before writing this book, I felt what happened to me at age twelve was the worst possible trauma that could have ever happened. But as I circulated my earlier drafts, I heard stories from other women. Some of them were almost envious that I found a way to break up with the Wolf and stop the sexual abuse. They told me stories of being three and four years old, with no power.

They spoke of abusers who were trusted family members. Not only could these little girls not get away, but they also didn't even have words for what was happening to them. When old enough to tell a parent, they were often met with disbelief.

I've realized it's not a competition, though. Any kind of rape and sexual abuse is traumatic, no matter the age, no matter the circumstances. Those of us who have experienced it in any form have been traumatized. It's a simple fact: trauma is trauma. We can't really compare and say one kind is worse than another. Trauma affects people differently, and people deal with trauma in different ways.

People do have different resiliency to trauma. Despite my family's limitations, I think their steadfast love for me helped make me resilient. At least my family was a safe place, a place where I knew I would never be abused.

I recently read the book *The Body Keeps the Score*. In a chapter titled "Inescapable Shock," the author, Dr. Bessel van der Kolk, describes a scientific experiment that was done on dogs. Animal lovers, be prepared to have your hearts broken.

In the study, a group of dogs was kept locked in cages and shocked repeatedly, while other groups of dogs weren't shocked. All the dogs were then put in cages, but the doors were left open. The researchers then shocked all the dogs. The dogs that had never been shocked before flew through the open doors and out of the cages to get away from the shock. The group previously shocked lay in their cages and continued to take the shocks. They whimpered and defecated and never left the cages, even though the doors were wide open. In the end, the researchers bodily dragged the dogs through the open doors to get them to understand they could escape the shocks. Teaching the shocked dogs that they could leave through the open cage door and not get shocked was nearly impossible.

The conclusion Dr. van der Kolk made was that like these traumatized dogs, many people with a history of trauma don't take action when they have opportunities to get to freedom. Trauma has become so "normalized" for them that they simply continue to take it. They don't have any coping mechanisms that help them to escape.

My family may have been dysfunctional, but they were not abusive. In a similar way, my relationship with God may have been mistaken and confused, but it was still a reality that had given me strength all through my childhood. Trauma did not seem normal to me. This meant that when I caught a glimpse of how it would be without the shame, guilt, and dirty feelings, I leapt through the open door. I broke up with the Wolf and was free.

However, trauma does stay with you, and it stayed with me. Many people who have experienced rape and sexual abuse have

PTSD (post-traumatic stress disorder). This means that they continue to relive the trauma even after it is over. It continues to shape their perception of reality.

The symptoms of PTSD usually start within a month of the traumatic event, but sometimes symptoms might not appear until years after the event. These symptoms can cause big problems with people's relationships, as well as their work lives. They can interfere with a person's ability to go about normal daily life.

One of the major symptoms of PTSD is memories that intrude on your life and get in the way of enjoying life fully. Sometimes the memories may be so sharp and clear that they feel as though you are experiencing the trauma all over again. (These are known as flashbacks.) Memories may also spill over into your sleep and cause nightmares. Triggers—such as smells, sounds, or certain situations—can bring the trauma's terrible emotions rushing back again.

PTSD can make people unable to relax and enjoy life, because they're constantly on guard, prepared for danger to strike at any moment. They may be easily frightened or startled, and they may have trouble sleeping. They might get angry easily or become aggressive.

Left untreated, PTSD can cause poor self-concept, depression, addiction, self-destructive behaviors, and even suicide. It can hinder a person's ability to form close relationships. People who experience PTSD can blame themselves and feel overwhelming guilt and shame. Those who experience these symptoms need to get professional help from a counselor or therapist. The passage of time can help, but sometimes PTSD may never fully go away without professional help.

Numbing is another common way to deal with the memory of trauma. Unfortunately numbing may numb you to all your life experiences so you take very little pain but also very little pleasure from your life. Numbing is a coping technique that I've experienced firsthand.

Several years ago, after I'd gone through a divorce, an acquaintance started showing up at my workplace and my new house because he was "in the area." He helped me set up a new basketball hoop for my son and did other "helpful" things. He was married, and I was also acquainted with his wife, so I didn't think much of it. One day, after he'd done another little helpful task, I offered him some water. As he drank it, he leaned into me and brushed my cheek with his hand. I went numb. In fact, I stopped breathing. I couldn't speak, and I felt my face go blank. "Come on," he said with a grin, "give me a sign here."

I took his glass from him and showed him out, all with the emotional state of a robot. After he left, I was quiet and self-absorbed for hours. I went through the motions of spending time with my kids and doing nightly chores, but emotionally, I had simply left. I stayed like that for several days, going about my daily life while feeling completely numb.

I finally got back on track when I told my counselor what happened. Taking about it and getting her reassurance that he was at fault, not me, made me able to put the episode into perspective. I went back to normal (and I never returned any of his calls again).

I never expected that would be how I would react to unwanted male attention, but sometimes, past trauma sends you into automatic pilot for a while. You may have heard when you get scared, your fight-or-flight response gets triggered—but there is a third option. You can fight, flight, or freeze. Numbing is a freeze response to intense anxiety.

Dissociating, which is when there's a break in how your mind handles information, is a step up from numbing. Dissociation makes you feel that you're not connected to your thoughts, feelings, and surroundings. It can affect your sense of identity and your perception of time. It can make you feel detached from your body, so much so that you may not even notice your body's pain responses. It's another coping mechanism for handling severe trauma.

I mentioned earlier that my coping skills run toward minimizing and rationalizing. When I broke up with the Wolf, I spun a story that I was too young and just wasn't ready for dating. I then proceeded to be very bright and cheerful around my friends and especially my family. I acted as though both the relationship and the breakup were no big deals. This made me seem mature for my age and quite grounded for a thirteen-year-old. My mom ate it up and didn't question me at all. *I* even ate it up. Remember, I didn't think I had been raped or sexually abused; I had been told, "Boys can't help themselves," and it was my job to keep myself safe, so I told myself I had made a mistake—one that I would never repeat.

This led to another way I coped: by becoming hypervigilant about my own sexual desires. Every boy I dated after that met a very sexually controlling Amber. I would decide ahead of time how far I would go with a guy. Would I hold hands? Would I kiss? Would I French kiss? Would I allow him to touch me? I never wanted to be caught unprepared again. I set boundaries with myself and stuck to them like glue. After all, I believed I was to blame for what had happened—so it was up to me to do the fixing.

And then I rationalized. I told myself, "Okay, I made a mistake, but I was young. Mistakes are going to happen. That's how you learn. I said I was sorry to the Wolf and he accepted my apology and condolences, so I have no reproach on that front. God knows the truth, but I'll just steer clear of God for a while and maybe in time I'll be forgiven. It wasn't so bad. I mean, I finked out on the marrying part and all, but I'm young, and everyone makes mistakes. It's like my mom said, all you can do is say you are sorry and make amends and let time heal your wounds. Time will pass, and things will feel better."

And eventually, they did. A little.

Coping skills help you cope. They make you feel better, at least in the short run.

Some people get drunk or high; they cope by checking out for a while.

Some people cut themselves.

Some people go numb.

Some people clean their houses incessantly.

Some people find new people to have sex with so they feel desirable.

Some people seek counseling and clarity.

Some people pray or meditate.

Some people paint pictures, make music, or write poetry.

There are a lot of ways people can cope. Some ways help you learn and grow from the trauma, but other coping methods can keep you stuck in self-destructive behaviors. You may need a therapist to help you identify your own coping behaviors—and then determine whether they are truly helping you or hindering you.

My initial coping mechanisms—minimizing and rationalizing—set me up to be victimized again.

Thirteen

Victimization

Instead of blaming the Wolf and dealing with my grief over being hurt by someone I loved and trusted, I took the blame and minimized and rationalized it away. Since I was the one to blame, I didn't feel wary of guys. So long as I kept my sexual boundaries in place, I still trusted that people were good and no one was out to harm me. I mean, why would anyone want to harm me? I'm nice and pleasing and vulnerable and over-compliant. Who wouldn't like that?

Well, I know who *would* like it. Other wolves, who saw the same personality traits in me at age eighteen that I had at age twelve.

One night when I was about twenty years old, I went to dinner with my girlfriends, and we ended up discussing the "date rape" drug called Rohypnol. If someone slips it into your drink or food, it's called being "roofied." As we were discussing the topic, someone asked if any of us thought that it had ever happened to us.

I got quiet and then said, "I think it did happen to me." I went on to tell them the following story.

When I was eighteen, I was asked to accompany a seemingly very nice guy, Steve, who I knew from the health club, to an out-of-town wedding. We planned to stay the night at a Super 8 Motel with two queen-size beds. He was nice and handsome, but I made it clear there would be no sex or even kissing or hand-holding at this point in our relationship because we were just friends. He agreed, and I thought he was quite the gentleman.

Then at the wedding, his friend made a sly comment about the Super 8 Motel and how that was going to be an "interesting 8mm film to watch." This seemed a very odd comment, but I figured the guys were talking about something private.

And that was the last thing I remembered until I was home the next afternoon, sitting on the sofa, fully dressed and petting my cat. I had no memory of the end of the wedding, the ride to the motel, getting ready for bed, getting up the next morning, or the long ride home in the car. This didn't scare me at first because I didn't even realize I couldn't remember the evening. I just checked the time and went about my day from there.

But a day or two later, a strange thing happened that made me wonder. I saw Steve at the club. He ducked his head, wouldn't meet my eyes, and barely said hi to me. He quit the gym right after, and I never saw or spoke to him again. I wondered if I had said or done something to offend him—but as I searched my memory, that is when I realized that no matter how much I tried or thought about it, my memory went straight from the reception to me petting my cat at home the next day.

I never drank alcohol or used drugs, and I'd only drank soft drinks that night. Of course, this scared me—but I also went straight to my old friends minimizing and rationalizing. Surely, if something bad had happened, I'd remember it. My body wasn't hurt, so nothing must have happened.

This category of rape can be very hard to process because the drugs have literally not allowed your brain to form long-term memories. There are many stories of college girls who went out to dinner and woke up hours later in their beds with no memory of what happened.

Women who have this experience often act like nothing happened and don't look into it further. They hardly ever press charges, because they can't make a coherent statement about what happened. Also, many people blame the victim. Or they accuse her of making things up.

I am not making up any of this book. I did fit a profile, and I attracted more than one wolf in my young life. Since I felt safe with my hypervigilant approach to my sex life, I felt Steve would honor our agreement and sleep in his own bed at the motel; I thought I was in control. I never even dreamed a scenario where a drug would cause me to lose my control.

I think some wolves prefer to be elusive.

Still, I hate to apply the word "victim" to myself, even though it's appropriate. Another word occurs to me, however, one I learned the summer before college when I worked at a game trailer at a fair. This was the game where if you pop a balloon with a dart, you get a prize. When I was being trained for this job, they called people who might play the game "marks." As in, "When you see a mark walking by, call out to them and make conversation, like, 'Oh I love that shirt!' or, "Would your little one like to try? It's easy!'" Then, hopefully, the person walks over to your booth, where you convince them with a cheerful smile that they should spend $5.00 for three darts and try to win a prize.

I feel like "mark" is a better description of a sexual abuser's victim. When the wolves of the world saw me, they saw an easy mark.

There have been studies done on purse-snatchers in prison that illustrate this concept. A hundred convicted purse-snatchers were shown a video of people walking on a street, at a fair, and in a mall. All the convicts identified the *same exact* few people they would try to assault and steal purses from. When asked why they picked these people, they all said they were easy targets. They could tell by the way the women held their purses, how they walked (not confident, heads down), and their overall physical size, shape, and demeanor. Basically, they were easy "marks."

And that's what I was. My coping mechanisms helped me survive—but they made me continue to be an easy mark. I had a lot of processing I still needed to do before I could truly heal.

Fourteen

Processing and Healing

A therapist I know talks about processing trauma as being a little like metabolizing food. We have to break the trauma down into its pieces, so that we can "digest" what happened. As long as it remains a huge, terrifying chunk of memory, it will continue to be stuck inside us. Processing allows us to learn from it and move on.

While writing this book, I have been processing the rape and subsequent abuse to understand better the dynamics of it all taking place. I've been reading and studying the terminology, recognizing my own experiences as I've consumed the therapeutic literature.

To start with, my counselor had me look up *Stockholm's syndrome*:

> *Stockholm syndrome is a psychological condition that occurs when a victim of abuse identifies, and attaches or bonds, positively with their abuser.*

Yes, that fits me, doesn't it?

Then let's talk a bit about the Wolf. He was a child molester, not a pedophile. Understanding the differences between the two has also helped me process what happened to me.

Many child molesters are, in fact, pedophiles, and many pedophiles are child molesters. But they are not necessarily one and the same. A pedophile is sexually attracted to children. Many people with pedophilia hate their desires and do not carry them out for moral reasons. Pedophilia is a psychiatric disorder, not a crime—unless it is acted on. Child molesters, however, have committed a crime by engaging in illegal sexual activity, of any kind, with children. They may be motivated by sexual desire—but they may also be motivated by power and control. That's the Wolf.

He also was a narcissist. Most child molesters and rapists are. They lack the empathy most people have that would make them feel shame or guilt over hurting someone else, especially a child. So just the fact that he was wanting to hurt a child would indicate a lack of shame, guilt, or empathy. He even gave me a birthday card with his signature on it stating how I should keep it because he would be famous someday. He gave me several "narcissistic slaps," which are cutdowns designed to undermine the victim's confidence (for example, commenting on my gaining weight and smelling like fish, or talking behind my back about my acne).

Narcissists are really good at finding a person's "hook" and then using it to gain control. With me, the Wolf used the idea that after the rape I was a "bad girl"; he held out the carrot stick of a continuing relationship that would lead to marriage, allowing God to forgive me for having sex so young. That was my hook. The Wolf knew just how to use my own beliefs to trap me into several more months of abuse.

For a different girl, it might be a different hook. My dad, for example, showed signs of narcissism, and he would threaten my mom that he would kill himself if she ever left him. That was her "hook," since she could never bear the thought of being responsible for his death. My dad's father had committed suicide, which made the threat that much more realistic. So even though my dad got voted out of our house when I was young, he never was really out of our lives. I finally understood why he was at the breakfast table every morning, showered and shaved and smoking a cigarette, talking my mother's ear off while she got me ready for school. Until the day he died, she loaned him money, bought him cars, bought him buildings for his recycling dreams, and had breakfast with him almost every morning to hear his plans.

Also, narcissists are predictable, beaming with charm so you feel like the sun is shining on you. They put you so high on a pedestal that you have to look down to see heaven. That is a narcissistic trait called "love bombing." It always happens at the beginning, while the narcissist is still determining what your hook is. Then, once he's got you, he starts with the sly cutdowns. Meanwhile, you are scrambling to get the sunshine back and bending over backward to please him—and this is just how he likes it. Power and control. Narcissistic abuse follows this same predictable cycle: love bombing, hook, criticisms, and finally moving on to the next target.

When I decided I had had enough abuse and broke up with the Wolf, I probably shocked the hell out of him. I doubt he could have figured on me telling God to "go hang" so that I could get control of my own sex life.

Geez, I was thirteen and I had a sex life I had to manage. Have you looked at a thirteen-year-old lately? When I taught dance for seven years after college, I always paid special attention to my twelve- and thirteen-year-old students. They are still babies. Princesses, little angels who like to wear shirts with hearts and flowers and, for crying out loud, rainbows on them!

They draw pictures of horses in tutus, and they give the drawings to their dance teacher to pin up on the studio mirrors. They practice cartwheels in the front lawn. They make up cheers and wiggle and bounce around the place like Tigger from *Winnie the Pooh*. They still think farts are funny.

That little kid who was so sensitive she cried anytime she did something the first time away from her mother? That was me. I also cried again and again at any story of babies losing their mothers or losing their way. I literally cried when I spilled my milk, and I often cried and wanted to come home when I tried to sleep at a friend's or cousin's house. (Bless my mom who always came and got me at 11 pm or midnight.) I loved stories where being honest and doing good paid off in the end, just like it should.

All that abuse, the lying and sly cutdowns, the smell, the trip to Planned Parenthood, and the certainty that everyone at the studio was talking about me—well, it was all torment. But mostly, the worst thing by a long shot, was feeling so ashamed and guilty before God. I was constantly praying:

> *I am so sorry, God. I am sorry, God. How will You forgive me, God? I had sex so young, God. I am no longer a virgin, God. I can never be an honorable wife unless it's with the Wolf, God. Make me feel love for him again, God, make me like this, God. Is spending my life not*

liking sex my punishment for having sex so young, God? The Wolf doesn't seem to like me as much as he did before—is that my punishment? Will he not marry me? What should I do, God? I want to be a good girl again. I want to please You, and I am trying to please him, and I just am so sorry I got myself into this mess and my mother warned me—boys just can't help themselves— but I went and ignored her every word and here I am in the worst possible place, God.

This interior monologue never stopped. It was the constant background to my life all during my time with the Wolf.

The night of the birthday sex, followed by crying in the bathtub, something cracked inside of me. Or maybe it's the other way around. Maybe something came together. I was ready to go unloved by God and unloved by anyone, so long as I no longer had to experience the soul-crushing agony of so much shame and sorrow. Despite my shame, despite my certainty that God would never forgive me, I took a step for *me*. I stood up for me. I believe my Soul Mate was right there with me, nudging me along to do the right thing for *me*.

But that didn't mean I wasn't still confused. What do you do when you screw up? You say you are sorry. You take responsibility for the screwup and try to make amends. At thirteen, I had already learned all that. I knew what I had to do. Unfortunately, I was still a child and very confused about who was doing the hurting and who should be saying they were sorry.

So when I broke up with the Wolf, I took full responsibility. I told him I was sorry, but I was just too young. I asked him to forgive *me.* I tried to make amends by asking if we could continue to be friends.

At least I managed to end the sexual abuse, although trying to remain "friends" with my abuser left me open for emotional abuse for a few more years. Not the best plan, but a plan that my sensitive self could survive.

Still, I got at least a glimpse of what it would be to be free from shame and sorrow. That was the real God talking, the Soul Mate who had never left me. The nonsense beliefs that had entrapped me, about marriage and virginity and what honorable meant, what "real love" was—no, those lies did not come from God. Deep inside, despite all my confusion, my soul knew that freedom from guilt and shame and sorrow was pure God speaking. My soul was shining bright as ever. And she still managed to hear God speak, even in the middle of the emotional crapstorm of my life.

But despite the presence of my Soul Mate, processing sexual abuse doesn't happen all at once. It comes in stages.

A friend of mine who read my story told me about her own experience of sexual abuse, which happened when she was a preschooler. At that age, she didn't have the words to label what was happening to her, and like me, she had no adult to help her make sense of the experience. She went through life feeling dirty and ashamed, without fully understanding why, until she was nearly fifty—at which point, she described her experiences out loud for the first time. When she did so, it became finally clear to her that she had been sexually abused. Only then, could she begin to truly heal. That process has taken years and is still ongoing a decade later.

Although my situation was very different, I went through a similar ongoing process. At first, because I never viewed what happened as rape and sexual abuse, I didn't feel like I had been victimized. Instead, I felt I had been really stupid. I thought to myself, *I got myself into that mess, I got myself out of it, and now I just have to deal with the consequences.*

I stopped talking to God for several long years. After all, God knew the whole "truth" about me being a "bad girl" and having sex too young. God knew it and I knew it, and I wasn't ready to have the Divine light shining so brightly on me anymore.

I think a lot of us who have experienced sexual abuse do that. Because we feel so ashamed, we try to duck our heads, hide our hearts, and evade God's sight. Of course, by doing so, we also limit our lives and make them a lot narrower. It's as though we think that by keeping to a narrow little strip of thoughts and experiences we'll be safe from the darkness we know is inside of us. We're terrified of having to face it.

Healing from my experiences with the Wolf has been a lifelong process that is still continuing. In my twenties, a counselor told me that what happened to me was rape: that I was raped and sexually abused. She assured me that it wasn't my fault. I went through the stages of grief, starting with denial for a very long time. Eventually, I agreed I had "been taken advantage of," but I still couldn't apply the word *rape* to myself.

A decade later, my counselor once again brought up the rape and insisted we needed to address it again. We read and did the exercises in the book *The Courage to Heal: A Guide for Woman Survivors of Child Sexual Abuse.* By the time we were done with the book, I felt I had adequately addressed the topic. I was tired of working with it. I wanted to put it to rest in my life, so that I could move on.

Then, in my forties, I had the dream about the Soul Mate. This sparked me to begin writing my story, and eventually, this turned into another revisit to my experience with the Wolf.

And yet I resisted the idea that this book is about rape. Was I still minimizing? Dissociating? I kept insisting that I wanted the book to be about what I had learned about God—and yet the Wolf kept intruding into the story. Finally, I was forced to acknowledge that my counselor had been right: I still hadn't fully processed the rape. I hadn't completely healed. As I continued to write, however, I gained more insights. I began to truly digest the meaning of my story, to finally metabolize it. My Soul Mate was at work again in my life, prompting me to take the necessary steps toward a more complete healing.

What I have come to realize is that all of us experienced some form of wounds when we were young, and as result, in some way or another, most of us feel we are not good enough. We drag those hurt little kids with us into every situation, and we perceive aspects of our adult lives through their eyes.

Even though I am an adult now, there is still a part of "little Amber" I carry with me. This is the same little Amber who watched her house burn down at age five when no one in her family met her at the safe spot, and the little Amber who spent a summer watching bruises heal on her previously perfect thighs and upper arms, the little Amber who felt nothing but disgust for her own fishy-smelling body.

There is something I would like to say to her.

Fifteen

Forgiving Yourself

Before I could even think about forgiving the Wolf, there was another person I needed to forgive. I needed to forgive little Amber.

And so I sat down and wrote these words to her:

Little Amber, I forgive you for getting caught in a trap set by an older male who never felt love or cared for you, but only wanted to control and hurt you.

I would like to thank you for your willingness to believe the good in people and your unbridled joy in God and life and animals and Nature, and your readiness to forgive and accept people's shortcomings. I appreciate your stick-to-it-ness when you perceive a problem that can be solved and be made better somehow, and your desire to want to help heal people.

I love you, little Amber, and you have my free and full forgiveness. I am saying goodbye to you with love and a glad heart!

I need to remember that although some children, like me, may be easier "marks" than others, they are not to blame. Only their abusers bear that burden. These children are truly "little sweethearts."

Let's think about that. The children I'm calling "little sweethearts" are basically just good kids. They are generally eager to please, nonaggressive, trusting, and naïve. They have not a clue of the dangers that are about to befall them.

Everyone loves special attention, to be singled out, and our little sweethearts are no exceptions. They may in fact just eat it up! Maybe, like me, they are loved and not abused at home, but there are still likely to be some holes in their upbringing.

My dad was an alcoholic, while my mother excused his drinking and actually gave him money for beer and cigarettes any time he asked. My mother was an enabler. The message I received was that it was easier to give in to him than argue.

I got a zillion other little messages too. Like when I was seven and there was a school open house and the teacher gave out Charm lollipops. One kid didn't like his flavor and pitched a bit of a fit. My mom immediately said, "Amber, trade with him so he is not upset," and I did. I was a little sweetheart who obeyed my mom easily—and she was teaching me to be a people-pleaser. It may not seem like a big deal, but many messages I got were along the same lines: "If someone is upset around you, you need to try and make them feel better. It's your responsibility." It started to feel like this was my purpose in life: look for unhappy people and try to fix their unhappiness.

But I can't blame the little sweetheart that I used to be. She was just a good kid doing the best she could. I don't want her to run my life anymore, though. And the only way to let her go was to forgive her.

As I said goodbye to little Amber, I realized I was finally ready to be an adult. Forgiving little Amber allowed me to let go of that little sweetheart as the filter through which I perceived my grown-up life. Now I could also let go of some of the defenses and coping skills the little sweetheart had developed. These were useful for a time; they helped little Amber survive—but now I am ready to use more effective methods of coping (and I want to teach them to my daughter as well). Never again will I say, "Maybe this is a blessing in disguise," as a way to excuse hurtful behaviors from others. I have learned about setting healthy boundaries.

Sixteen

Boundaries

My mom thought she was teaching me to be nice—but really, she just showed me the best way to be a doormat and not complain. She had a lot of ways to teach this. "You catch more flies with honey than you do with vinegar," was one of her favorite sayings, along with, "How would you feel if that were you?" and, "Treat other people how you want to be treated."

All of this is great advice and a good way to live—if you know where the line between heathy and unhealthy is. She didn't. So I was never taught that it's okay to say "no." Or that it's okay to stand up for yourself. She certainly never told me, "If anyone's touch makes you uncomfortable, start pitching your own hissy fit about it!"

Child molesters can spot little sweethearts like me a mile away. They are easy targets that eat up the special attention, easily get lured away from the group, and won't blab when the adult starts hurting them. They are vulnerable, need approval, and are over-compliant. They don't have the boundaries they need to keep them safe. Many little sweethearts will in fact feel like it was their own fault. I sure did.

Having good boundaries with other people keeps you safe and in harmony with yourself. When you have good boundaries, you know if someone is crossing a line and trying to hurt you. You will feel sad, angry, and used if a person does manage to cross that line. You will tell them you don't like that. In an honest, caring relationship, the other person will feel remorse that they upset you and try to change.

But many little sweethearts were raised to not have many or any boundaries. Mothers and fathers think they are teaching their children to be kind and "turn the other cheek" by instantly forgiving another person's hurtful actions. When it comes to safety, that advice can get you involved in abusive relationships.

My mother herself had very few boundaries with anyone, even her children. Even though there were a few rules at home—be honest, don't steal, treat others how you want to be treated—she broke many of these rules herself when she told "little white lies" so no one would get mad at her.

For example, once when I was invited to spend the night at a friend's house, I accepted—but later, I got an invitation to go roller-skating with a friend I liked better. My mom told a "little white lie" for me and said I had a fever and she didn't think I should spend the night with the first friend. Although I had fun at the roller rink, I ended up with a knot in my stomach, afraid the first girl would find out I didn't really have a fever.

Another example would be the many, many times we told "little white lies" to not upset my father. This included things like telling my dad we got lucky at the thrift store and got a brand new shirt for me for just a few dollars, when really we paid retail price at a department store. My mom said it was okay to tell this lie so my dad wouldn't be upset she had spent money on me and had less money to give to him for beer and cigarettes.

This put a different knot in my stomach, especially since my dad often yelled, loudly and with great sincerity and emphasis, "Be honest!" I worried a lot about what I would do if my dad asked me about the shirt. I ended up putting the shirt in the bottom of my dresser drawer and never wore it, although I had badgered my mom quite a lot to buy it for me.

Another example of confusing or no boundaries came from my dad. He did frequently yell at us kids to be honest, but both he and my mom, with us kids in tow, would sometimes go out at night to loot abandoned houses out in the country.

My mom frequently tells this "funny story" about how when I was very little, just three years old, we were going through an abandoned house and I found a dirty stuffed animal I wanted to take home. My dad said it was too dirty. I whined and said, "But you and Mom are bringing home all this dirty stuff." He was evidently in a good mood and my logic struck him funny; I was allowed to keep the dirty stuffed toy.

He also drove a taxi cab as a mostly steady job for many years and would give me rides to or from dance class if my mom or sister couldn't get me. Several times, I watched him count his money from the shift, put it into two separate piles, and hide one pile in an inner vest pocket. When I asked why he did this, he said, "I always like to take my tuck before I get back to the garage." I don't think this "tuck" was just his tips. So even though he said, "Be honest!" to us kids, he clearly didn't follow the same rules.

My mother would be what the therapeutic community would call an enabler and a co-dependent. She was an over-giver, always putting my dad and other people over herself. She thought this was the way women "should" be, and if I called her on it and pointed out she wasn't getting fair treatment from people, she would always say, "Geez, Amber, you can be so selfish. It's good to give to others." As my mother seemed to be really smart compared to other adults I knew, I took that criticism to the bank. I learned to "people please," so it's not really a surprise that when I was raped and abused, I just let it all happen. The Wolf wanted something from me—and I didn't want to be selfish, right? I didn't want him to be unhappy.

I still struggle today with saying "yes" when I would rather say "no." I get upset and tense if I perceive anyone being mad at me, and I often find myself giving in to the demands of my children, my friends, and my husband, just so no one will think I'm being selfish.

But although I still struggle with boundaries, I do know now that they are essential and healthy. We have the right to set a personal boundary anytime someone's actions or words make us uncomfortable—and we don't need to justify that to anyone. Our personal boundaries are what keep us safe and comfortable. They come in a couple of different forms.

Internal boundaries are between you and you. They help you regulate the relationship you have with yourself. Another term for them might be "self-discipline." These boundaries help you to manage time effectively. They allow you to regulate your own emotions (rather than allowing your emotions to control your life), and they give you impulse control, which allows you to avoid dangerous and hurtful behaviors.

External boundaries are between you and other people. They allow you to recognize where other people's needs stop and yours begin. You decide what these boundaries are; no one else can tell you what is okay and not okay in your relationships.

My counselor uses this example for external boundaries. Say in a relationship you pretend you are on a football field. Everything from the 0- to 50-yard line is your space and your rules. The opposite 0- to 50-yard line is the other person's space and their rules. You don't push into their 30-yard line without their permission and say-so. And they do not push into your 30-yard line without your permission and say-so. Of course, as relationships develop and get more intimate, you may want them closer and so you set a new boundary line; for example, your close relationship with your husband and kids probably hovers around the 10- or 20-yard line—but only with your say-so. You get to decide how close people can come to you.

For those of us who have difficulties with boundaries, it can be hard to recognize where the boundary lines are—but with practice, it gets easier. If people are not respecting your external boundaries and blowing right past and into the 20-yard line, you will get a knot in your stomach. You'll feel uncomfortable. Learn to respect that feeling. Take it seriously. Don't rationalize it away, and don't minimize it. If you're like me, you may hate confrontation; you may not want to hurt people's feelings. But boundary lines are essential not only for your own health but also for healthy relationships with others.

I'll be honest: I still work on this constantly. I still struggle to have good external boundaries. My natural tendency is to include anyone I perceive is feeling left out, even if they are not a particular friend of mine. I'll also take the smallest piece of steak or the burnt vegetables, and leave the better ones for my husband and children, so no one gets upset. My husband recently brought it to my attention that I will even endlessly inconvenience myself for our dog, throwing the ball past the point that I am enjoying it, or letting her jump up on my lap when I am trying to work. Like I said, I am still learning to set and keep healthy boundaries.

But I do know for a fact that having good boundaries really is the only way to fly for having healthy and harmonious relationships. They're what protect us from abuse—and teaching them to our children will prevent them from becoming "marks" for the abusers out there who are looking for their next victim.

I'd made a lot of progress by the time I figure out all this. And then, just when I had things all wrapped up . . . God showed up again in a dream.

Seventeen

Another Dream

This book was all but finished. The audio tracks had been laid down, the cover art had been thought about and approved, and we were just crossing some t's and dotting some i's. I was learning how to design a website, and the finished art was only several weeks away. And then one night, I had another lucid dream.

Almost exactly one year had gone by since I started this book, and in that time I had read the Bible almost cover to cover. I was thinking about becoming a lay minister, and I was going to be giving a sermon at my church. For my sermon, I had picked Matthew 25:31–45 as my scripture text, what's commonly known as the story of the sheep and the goats. It's the one where

Jesus comes back at the end of days and separates good people (sheep) and bad people(goats), stating that the good people gave him food when he was hungry, water when he was thirsty, a room when he was homeless, clothes when he needed clothing, visited him when he was sick, and came to see him when he was in prison—but the bad people (goats) did none of those things. The piece had been buzzing around in my head for a while, and I liked it for a lot of reasons.

Although I was happy with my sermon and got the thumbs-up from my pastor, I had spent a lot of time thinking about hell and why it is even in the Bible. What kind of sadist burns their beloved children for all eternity? It just doesn't jive with the loving and nurturing and patient God I know and love. The past year's Bible study was literally the first time I had read the Bible. There were many questions like this one that had me wondering about God.

So here I am at two o'clock in the morning—and God shows up in my head.

Amber, you didn't like the sheep and the goat story?

Well, I answer, *I liked it a lot. So much I'm even doing my first sermon on it. It's just the part about the goats being banished to hell that I don't like. I don't think the goats should be left out.*

I'm a little nervous saying this to God, though I'm sure God already knows I don't want to believe in a Divinity who would leave people out.

God asks me, *What about this person?* In my dream, I see a really bad person, instantly dislikable: conniving, a cheater ... But as I see him being thrown like a broken ragdoll over a cliff into oblivion—discarded, never to return—I want to grab him, pull him back to safety.

No, I tell God. *"I don't want him to be left out!"*

Well, what about this person? God asks me, and this time I see a woman blowing cigarette smoke into her baby's face. I watch as she yanks her kids by their arms, and I can tell she never wanted children and resents the ones she has now. But as she is about to get tossed over the edge of that cliff, I start crying because she has a look of total surprise on her face, like she never saw this one coming. I grab her arm and pull her back.

No! I don't want her left out! I shout, trying to drag her away from the cliff edge even though she is dead weight and not helping at all.

What about this one? God asks me, and I see a guy I know is a sex trafficker. He's shifty-eyed, cruel, despicable. And yet I sob, *No! No! Not him either! I don't want any of them to be left out."*

Why? God asks.

Still crying, I say, *They were all good once. They were all the bright shiny beautiful souls* You *made. They are still that.*

I realize I believe what I'm saying. I truly do.

You have kept their souls perfect, I say to God, *no matter what got them through this life.* My nose is running, and my childlike logic is failing me, and yet I can't let this go. *I don't want to obey a God that leaves anyone out,* I say.

I feel bad questioning God, but I can't stop thinking about hell. It's not the sadistic pit of burning fire I am thinking of either; no, it's the years when I thought God had abandoned me and I was on my own. The years I didn't think I had a Soul Mate who was always on my side and rooting for me. The years I thought I was better off alone. If I had had to live cast out and alone without God's love for all eternity, I just can't imagine the sense of loneliness and not belonging. That would truly be hell. And it's something people really do experience in this life, cut off from God and love and connection.

I would drag each and every person I could find to safety if I could. I wouldn't let any of them be goats, abandoned in hell.

When I hear God speak again, the voice is very gentle. *That is how Jesus felt. That is why he chose to die. So no one ever gets left out.*

Now I am crying tears of relief. I can love, trust, and obey my God again. God makes sense after all.

And then God asks me, *What about the Wolf?*

I see the Wolf at age two or three in a baby tap-dance class, with shiny new tap shoes. He's so proud click-clicking away with the rest of the kids at the dance studio—and I see nothing but innocence in his face. I realize I don't want him to be left out either. Of course, I don't; I don't want anyone ever to be left out.

God says, *It's rallying time, Amber. Time to finish what you began—and you're one chapter short. You have a book to finish.*

That was the end of the dream. I woke up the next morning knowing that this book needed me to write a little more. It has been the hardest chapter to write, though.

The last time I saw the Wolf in person was almost twenty-five years ago. After I graduated from the dance studio at age eighteen, I didn't follow his life closely, so I don't know if he was happy or not. I think he won awards for choreography. I think his dance studio did well. From what I understand, he started being asked to choreograph and guest teach at workshops, teaching and judging at competitions.

But then, when I was twenty-three, I heard he had been arrested. I found the story in the newspaper: he had checked into a hotel with one of his thirteen-year-old students, where he had had sex with her. He pled guilty and was sentenced to some prison time. When he was released, he was labeled a sex offender and could no longer teach dance to children.

At that time that I had a new dance partner, and Brian and I were giving lessons and doing a couples' dance exhibition in a local hotel ballroom. I asked my old dance teacher, the Wolf's mother, if we could use her studio to practice and get ready for the exhibition. She said we could use the studio during the day, when no classes were going on.

So there we were, Brian and I, working on our routine and doing some lifts, trying to perfect a move called a "crow's nest" (which is easy if you get the timing and balance right—but leaves the girl sitting embarrassed like a lump on the floor if you don't). And in walks the Wolf, right onto the dance floor.

He looked like total crap. His clothes were dirty, and he was skin and bones. His shaggy hair made him look more wolfish than ever.

He said hi to me and crossed the floor to give me a hug. Practically paralyzed, I felt his hand land on my hip. It was an awkward hug with his hand on my hip that way, and it felt possessive, like I was still his somehow. He released me quickly, and I let it go (not wanting a confrontation, in typical Amber style).

Then he launched into an unsolicited diatribe about how he was a carpenter now because " those little bitches" had ruined his life. Not knowing what to say, I said nothing. Brian, completely confused, introduced himself. The Wolf must have felt uncomfortable, because he said he had a lot to do and left. We all went back to what we were doing, but I spent a lot of time venting to my husband later that night.

"Those little bitches ruined *his* life? Is he kidding me? Can he possibly be for real?"

At that point, I don't think I was ready to forgive the Wolf of anything. It had only been about a year or so since I had confided in a counselor what had happened to me. I had still been thinking I was at fault, that what the Wolf and I had was some sort of messed-up relationship I had agreed to when I was way too young. I was so ashamed of it, I could barely think about it, much less talk about it openly to anyone. But right around the time when he walked into the dance studio was when I was first accepting that what he had done to me was rape.

It was just not the right time to forgive him. I could barely wrap my head around the idea he had even wronged me. I needed to be able to see that, accept that, believe that, before I could begin to think about forgiveness.

This book's original title was *A Different Kind of Rape* because I just didn't know what to call what happened to me. The Wolf had carefully groomed me long before he tried to have intercourse with me. I've realized that the psychological part of what he did to me was truly worse than the physical acts of rape and sexual abuse.

He was sweet at first. He flirted with me in a very non-threatening, nonsexual way, pulling my ponytail and spinning me around and laughing and joking. He didn't make lewd jokes that made me uncomfortable; he made silly jokes that had me laughing. I felt at ease with him.

One time, as we all were walking down the stairs to class, he encompassed the back of my waist with one hand and said, "My goodness your waist is so tiny!" His touch was gentle, his tone respectful. I glowed inside because my teacher had noticed me and praised me. I was thrilled!

Then the love letters began, with lots of heart and flower stickers. They all said, "I love you"; some had heart-shaped erasers or pencils with hearts on them. I kept them as treasures in a shoebox under my bed and read and reread them many times. My mind was full of him. He grabbed my hand in secret and with intensity emanating from every cell in his body, all the way up to his face and in his eyes, he told me I was so "sweet" and "special," and he just couldn't stop thinking about me. I lay awake thinking about him all night.

He gave me secret chocolates or sticks of gum on the sly with a wink and a "shh, don't let anyone know." After a while, he began to brush my arm or push loose strands of hair back behind my ears. These new behaviors didn't send up red flags because they'd come along so gradually. My heart would race each and every time.

My feelings were 100 percent real—so why would I doubt the reality for him? When he kissed me the first time, it was sweet and gentle, with no pressure. I never felt any sixth sense of danger. You know how your mother told you to listen to your gut when it comes to trusting a man? Well, if anything my gut was telling me, "I want more!" It felt beautiful and wonderful; my blossoming sexuality was being stroked in all the right places.

He made me fall in love with him. He tricked me into thinking he loved me too. My love was sincere, but his love was twisted. And eventually, he used my love against me to hurt me. Somewhere inside me, some wires got crossed. I no longer believed I was clean or good or loveable.

That is what has been the hardest to forgive. Not the sex act. Taking my virginity, that was forgivable. But robbing me of my own sense of myself, making it so hard for me to uncross those wires—that was hard to let go.

When I try to put these feelings into words, I find myself picturing two containers inside of me. One is filled with sunshine and the other holds storm clouds. The sunshine expresses my self-worth, all the times I've felt good about myself, when I've been happy to simply be me—but those dull, grey storm clouds indicate my lack of self-worth, the part of me that is constantly seeking other people's approval to tell me if I'm good enough. The sunshine part of my heart is able to check myself out and see if I am doing a good job based on my own calculations. Meanwhile, the shadowy, cloudy part hands a ruler to other people and lets them measure me.

Those two containers hold other things as well. Before I met the Wolf, I had been busy, like most children, categorizing life into sunshine or storms. I knew that some things were "bad": lying makes people not trust you; stealing feels yucky; eating too many cookies makes your stomach hurt; hurting an animal makes you cry. As I got a little older I added something else to the "bad" category: sex when you are too young is wrong; sex before marriage is very wrong; probably all sex is just plain wrong. And while I was filling up the stormy container, I was also adding things to the sunshine container: people who are nice to you love you, butterflies remind me of God; you know when things are true; you can trust yourself; your mom really loves you; you make good decisions; you're a smart girl, you are a trustworthy person; people like you because you are honest, you don't lie, and you don't cheat. Things seemed so clear back in those days. I could separate the sunshine from the clouds so easily.

And then, within a matter of weeks, the Wolf made me drop my carefully thought-out containers. The sunshine and the shadows got so mixed together that it was hard for me to tell which was which. I could no longer tell if I was a good person or a bad one. I didn't know whether sex—and enjoying sex—was right or wrong.

I no longer trusted myself to make good decisions. I was especially insecure about my love relationships. Since I didn't dare measure them for myself, I gave my ruler to many other people. I asked my friends what they thought about my love relationships. I asked my mom and my sister what they thought, and I asked the guys I was dating what they thought about my relationships with them. I even asked new guys who wanted to date me what they thought about the current guy I was dating. Basically, I gave my ruler away to everyone. I let everyone else measure the worth of my relationships, but I didn't dare measure them for myself. I trusted everyone but myself to decide what was best for me.

The Wolf left me feeling so dirty that I lost my connection with my own inner guide, my soul seat. I almost never talked to God about my love life. I felt too ashamed.

Of course, all love relationships are challenging. But whenever I faced any problems in a relationship, it would get mixed up with those bad left-over feelings from the Wolf. Again and again, my memories of that damn Wolf made my romantic life a big weepy mess. My sunshine and clouds were still so mixed up that I couldn't separate them. I just couldn't see anything clearly anymore.

And now? Well, I just turned fifty. It's been thirty-seven years since the Wolf took away my innocence. I think that's probably long enough to let him call the shots in my life. It's time to finally walk away from his power over me.

After my dream, I started researching what experts say about trauma and forgiveness. I found out that while most religions talk a lot about forgiveness, psychologists and other researchers just started really looking at it about thirty years ago. They determined that forgiveness isn't so much an emotion or a behavior as it is a mindset.

I discovered that forgiving is not the same thing as forgetting or pardoning. I will never forget what the Wolf did to me, and I can never say that what he did was okay. To do either of those things wouldn't be healthy. It would undo all the work I've done over the years to come to terms with what happened.

Dr. Bob Enright, a psychologist at the University of Wisconsin, is one of the pioneers in forgiveness research. His conclusions taught me some important things that have helped me make sense out of my dream about the Wolf. I learned that one common but mistaken belief is that forgiveness means letting the person who hurt you off the hook. But, Dr. Enright explained, forgiveness is not the same as justice.

Another researcher, Everett Worthington, was in the middle of his forgiveness studies when his mother was murdered (in my mind, that gives him a lot of credibility). He wrote that forgiveness doesn't require reconciliation; in other words, we don't have to make up and make nice with the person who hurt us—in fact, we probably shouldn't, because doing so could put us in danger either physically or emotionally (or both). But, Worthington, said we can still reach a place of empathy and understanding. That's what happened to me in the dream when I saw the Wolf about to be thrown into hell: I felt compassion for him. Forgiveness isn't about justice, and it isn't necessarily about any outer actions at all. "Forgiveness," Worthington said, "happens inside my skin."

Sometimes people feel as though being angry will make them stronger. When someone has abused us, I believe we definitely need to acknowledge and face our anger. But then we need to let it go, and forgiveness is the way we do that. Forgiveness won't make you weak, Worthington said; instead, it makes you physically and emotionally healthier.

Research has shown that forgiveness helps reduce anxiety, depression, and other major psychiatric disorders. It reduces stress (and stress can cause all sorts of physical issues, such as heart disease and high blood pressure). Forgiveness, the researchers found, contributes to higher energy levels and an improved immune system. It can even make us live longer.

Forgiveness can also help rebuild self-esteem, Dr. Enright said. When people allow their sense of injury to live on over the years, they hurt themselves far more than they do their abuser. In fact, they magnify the damage that the abuser did in the first place. "When you stand up to the pain of what happened to you and offer goodness to the person who hurt you," Dr. Enright said, "you change your view of yourself."

I can see the truth of all that in my own life. But forgiveness does take time, and honestly, I can't think of any way to rush it. So be patient with yourself if you're struggling with the idea.

But please don't give up! Forgiveness will allow you to get the last piece of your abuser out of your head so you can take back your own thoughts and stop obsessing. You'll be able to reclaim your peaceful sleep and stop having night terrors and panic attacks.

If you are reading this book and you are newly hurt, you may not be anywhere near the forgiveness stage yet. You have a lot to figure out. Your own healing and clarity is foremost. That's why I'm writing this book.

And don't think that the wolves of this world get off scot-free. Whether or not they're legally tried and brought to justice, they will in some way suffer the consequences of their actions.

When I was researching this book, I did a background check on the Wolf. He had just been arrested for a third time in Florida, this time for grand larceny. As I studied his mug shot, I thought, "I bet you dollars to donuts he is still telling people that someone else is to blame for ruining his life." One day, I hope he will own up to his own responsibility for making his life a mess.

But I can honestly say, "He's not my problem anymore. It's up to God to sort him out."

I feel so grateful for the sense of healing and closure I have now after my dream. I believe this really is the "final chapter" in my story about the Wolf. I hope you will one day reach your final chapter too.

I am so grateful that at the conclusion of this book, I can say, "Thank You, God! I'm so glad I'm not responsible for this man's life; I'm only responsible for my own journey with You." Now I can pray with a truthful heart, "Help the Wolf find his way to become a sheep, God. A real one, safe with You."

Afterword

In writing this book I have come to more fully understand the confusing part of my life that was marred by the Wolf. It wasn't just the summer when I turned thirteen that he damaged, but the years that followed as well, years of hyper-vigilance, self-control, shame, and needing to please others more than myself.

When I finished writing my story, I asked my mother to read it. I wanted to know if it would hurt her, and if she would be comfortable with me sharing stories of her and my father's parenting. Her reaction helped me realize I no longer felt ashamed. She read it and gave me permission to have it published.

The only advice she had was that I publish it under my maiden name rather than the name of my second husband, which I currently use. My mother went on to explain that my husband and his family are such good people that she didn't think I should sully their name and their family by publishing under their name.

At first, I took her advice to heart, but it didn't sit well. Then I figured out why. This book is not about *my* shame. I have none. I was just a little sweetheart who got trapped and used by someone in a position of power.

This story expresses my joy that I have finally put the past into perspective—and in doing so, I've restored my right and respectful relationship with God, my Soul Mate.

This story *is not* my shame. I have no shame. Not anymore.

Exercises

I am not a counselor, but I have learned a few things that have helped me heal, and I think it is safe to share them in this book. I would never encourage anyone to face their personal trauma without a trained professional to help them process it. You don't want to get retraumatized; you want to heal and feel better. So keep in mind that these exercises are not meant to replace therapy. They are intended only to comfort and strengthen you on your journey.

EXERCISE 1

Simply take a warm bath with 2 cups of salt and 2 cups of baking soda. Soak for 20 minutes. When you get out and dry off, you may feel drained—but then lie in the sun until you don't want to lie there anymore. If you can't lie in the sun, take a nap for as long as you stay asleep. This soothes you and recharges your energy field. You should feel revitalized and peaceful.

Many people who have experienced trauma will have chronic illnesses like lupus, chronic fatigue syndrome, fibromyalgia, and so on. Because you have kept the trauma within you, it is literally making you sick. This exercise is a simple way you can recharge your energy field once a week. It helps balance your core light.

It is always good to take time to take care of yourself. It is a signal to the little child inside of you that you are worth time and attention.

EXERCISE 2

Write some "wet pages" of your own. Tell the story of your personal trauma, with as many details as you can remember. It doesn't matter if you ever allow anyone else to read your writing. Writing frees up the left half of your brain and lets you reexperience your trauma with the nonjudgmental right side of your brain. If you are still holding beliefs that you were somehow responsible for your abuse, this exercise can help you see it in a non-self-judging way, which can be very freeing. Don't be afraid to cry as you realize that you didn't cause any of the abuse that befell you. You were in fact just a "little sweetheart" who was doing the best she could.

EXERCISE 3

I used this earlier in the book, in chapter 15. It's called the Forgiveness Exercise, and it is used to clear any grudge, sadness, or burden you may be holding in your energy field.

You may automatically assume that I will ask you to forgive your attacker. Well, that is up to you.

First, take a moment of silence and think about whomever you feel you are holding, in your own soul, with something against them. (When I did this exercise the first time, the person who came up was my mother; then, the second time I did it, it was "little Amber" whom I needed to forgive.)

Once you have a person in mind, say out loud:

<u>(Person's name)</u> *"I forgive you for* <u>(be specific)</u> *."*

"I would like to thank you for: _____."
(Although they may have done you wrong for a specific time, there may have been times they did you right. You may have learned something from them that is still useful to you today.)

If you love this person say out loud: *"I love you."* If you do not love this person say out loud, *"I do not love you, but you have my free forgiveness."*

Say out loud*: "If you die or I die, I would say goodbye with love* (if felt) *and a glad heart!*

Be sure to say goodbye to the person because you never know when death will come—and without saying goodbye, you may be leaving your own soul with unfinished business. If the person has already died, you can still do this exercise. In that case, it may be more helpful to say goodbye to a picture or memento of them. The forgiveness will still be released in your own soul (or energy field).

Have tissues present!

EXERCISE 4

Choose a theme song! Make it inspirational.

In my twenties, my theme song was "Tub-Thumping" by Chumbawamba: "I get knocked down, but I get up again! You are never gonna keep me down."

In my thirties, it was "Defying Gravity," from the musical *Wicked*: "I'm through with playing by the rules of someone else's game."

In my forties, it was "I Didn't Know My Own Strength" by Whitney Houston.

Currently, it is "It's in Every One of Us" by Davis Pomeranz: "Find your heart, Open up both your eyes."

What would your theme song be? Write down the lyrics. Explain the meaning they have for you. Be specific.

Alternatively, you could pick a poem, quote, or Bible verse that has a special meaning to you. Here are a few verses that have come to mean a great deal to me:

I will lift up my eyes to the mountains, from where shall my help come? My help comes from the Lord, who made Heaven and Earth. . . . He will keep your soul. The Lord will guard your going out and your coming in from this time forth and forever. (Psalm 121:1, 8)

You took a risk trusting Me, and now you're healed and whole. Live well, live blessed! (Luke 8:48)

Those who hope in the Lord will renew their strength. They will soar on wings like eagles: they will run and not grow weary, they will walk and not be faint. (Isaiah 40:31)

I have it all planned out—plans to take care of you, not abandon you, plans to give you the future you hope for. (Jeremiah 29:11)

Write your own verse or other quote on a notecard and place it where you will see it often. Repeat it frequently throughout the day.

EXERCISE 5

The last exercise is designed to help put you back in touch with both God and your own body.

You may already know that there is a place in your body that tells you right from wrong and good from bad. People say, "Trust your gut," or "I got a knot in my stomach and I knew there was something wrong," or, "I just can't stomach this." Although our guts can be tricked (as happened to me when the Wolf groomed me), when we *do* feel this tummy-twisting, it's almost always infallible. So if your gut tells you something isn't right, you can take it to the bank. It is a foolproof guide for setting boundaries, so that you have few regrets later on.

There is also another very special place that many people have not heard of, where you can talk to God. This is called your "soul seat." It is located in the middle of your chest right above your heart, on the inside. Next time you are praying, allow your hands to cover this spot. You will feel longing and yearning there. And when someone says that they feel like their "heart will burst with joy" or their "cup runneth over," it is actually that spot where they feel those sensations.

But you can feel remorse there too. It functions a little like a barometer, letting you know if your internal weather is sunny or stormy. When someone hurts you on the inside, however, that barometer can get out of whack. Or you may just shy away from even looking at it, like I did. It's hard to use it effectively to find your path or light your way if you are skirting it or avoiding it altogether.

But when you are traumatized and someone has hurt your body or damaged you emotionally, that spot can get damaged too. It can start to feel like an uncomfortable spot. A spot you don't want to show God anymore. Where shame resides. Where guilt lives. It damages your direct connection to God. It may make you want to lean away from God instead of turning toward the Source of life.

Have you prayed so hard for a yearning to be fulfilled? That is you knowing your path. Following it may not be a simple straight line, but following it will bring you to your heart's desire. When your communication with God is working properly, you can trust that feeling. God loves bringing people along a path right to their hearts' desire! God takes great joy in our happiness and wants good things for us all.

You might need to practice talking to God, however, if something harmful has happened to you and you need some healing. I am going to end this book by introducing one last exercise to help you reconnect to your internal communication with God. To get reacquainted with your "soul seat."

Imagine your soul looks like a moth or a butterfly. Is it big or little? Is it colorful? Does it have a pattern? Can you see it from far away or do you have to be really close to see it? Is it strong or fragile? If you can draw it, or find a picture of it on the Internet, paste it onto this page.

When you have a clear picture of what your soul as a butterfly or moth looks like, turn the page.

Now pretend to cup your hands and hold your butterfly inside. Tell God that you are holding the perfect soul you were created to be. Whisper your name to God as you tell the ways you have been hurt and are in need of some healing. God hears you when you do this. Your cupped hands are keeping you safe and quiet because God likes quiet, safe places to heal souls. God heals a soul by helping you remember the perfect soul you started as.

Can you remember a time you knew you were a shiny and beautiful soul? When was that?

You are still that. When you remember that, your healing will be well on its way. You will not hurt so much anymore.

Come to this page of healing anytime you need a quiet, safe place to rest your soul. Your healing hands will give you a resting place, and God will meet you inside, helping you remember that you are shiny and perfect. There is no other way for your soul to be.

When you are ready, turn the page

No one has seen your beautiful soul but God. What you whisper in this healing place only God hears; what you remember in the healing place, God knows. Your hands provide the safe quiet space for the healing.

I am going to tell you a truth: one day, you will not need the protection of healing hands to find a safe quiet place to be with God and remember who you are. That shiny perfect soul you were made to be.

There is a place another place you can go—when you are ready—but if someone really hurt you, it may not feel like a safe place. That is why it will be easier to turn into a butterfly and use your healing hands . . . and you can use them as much and for as long as you wish.

But if you feel ready to reconnect your shiny perfect soul directly to God, here is what you do.

Everyone has a quiet safe place inside them right above their heart. Your "soul seat." It is the place *your* hands protect when you pray. It is where you can communicate with God, soul to soul or heart to heart. You can continue your journey knowing you have a Soul Mate who is always with you and always rooting for you. Even if you try to leave for a while, your Soul Mate will never abandon you.

Blessings,
Amber

Definitions

Boundaries: A boundary marks a limit, and psychological boundaries define the line between behaviors that cause harm and behaviors that do not cause harm. These can be internal, protecting ourselves from our own harmful behaviors, such as eating or drinking too much, or they can be external boundaries, which protect us from others. The ideal way to live life is with mutual cooperation, but all of us have times when we must interact with others who are not cooperative and rather are hostile or manipulative; when that's the case, it is necessary to have strong boundaries to protect yourself. Boundaries are set consciously, to create healthy limits for relationships, protecting body, mind, and heart from the hurtful trespass of others.

Coping mechanisms: Sometimes called defense mechanisms, these were usually learned in childhood, and helped the individual survive abuse or neglect, but they are generally unconscious behaviors that are less than effective for adult life.

Dissociating: A **coping mechanism** that causes a break in how your mind handles information, which can make you feel disconnected from your thoughts, feelings, memories, and surroundings. It can affect your sense of identity and your perception of time. When you dissociate, you may forget things or have gaps in your memory. You may think the physical world isn't real or that you aren't real, or you may feel as though you are outside your own body. Emotionally, you may feel numb or detached, and you may be unaware of physical pain. Your sense of time may be altered; you might experience intense memories or fantasies that seem more real than what is actually going on around you.

Emotional numbing: A **coping mechanism** many people use when dealing with physical or emotional trauma, overwhelming stress, depression, or anxiety, which blocks the perception of emotional reactions.

Enabling: Actions taken, usually with the intention of helping a person or saving a relationship, that result in further harm, generally because the "help" (enabling behavior) only helps the person continue making poor choices, as well as avoiding natural consequences for their actions.

Enabler: You could think of an enabler as an "over-giver," helping and giving so much, and excusing such bad behavior, that the other person doesn't ever have a natural consequence to their problematic behavior.

Grooming: When someone builds a relationship, trust, and emotional connection with a child or young person so they can **manipulate**, exploit and abuse them. Children and young people who are groomed can be sexually abused, exploited, or trafficked. (Examples of the Wolf grooming me would be the "beary special" bear at Christmas time, twirling me around by my ponytail in a friendly almost family-like way, singling me out and using me for demonstrations in class, sending me secret notes, pushing my sexual boundaries gently at first, kissing and touching just a little and then building to more invasive touching and kissing over time, and braiding my hair, which though nonsexual, was very intimate touching.) Whether it's a priest, a coach, a cub scout leader, or a dance teacher, mothers and fathers feel safe leaving their children with the people who abuse children. So in a sense, these abusers spend time "grooming" the parents as well as the children they hope to **victimize**.

Hook: This is how the victimizer draws you in and then uses your own beliefs or fears to keep you in a relationship with them or "on the hook."

Love bombing: The practice of showering a person with excessive affection and attention in order to gain control or significantly influence their behavior. The love bomber's attention might feel good, but the motive is all about **manipulation**.

Manipulation: A type of social influence that aims to change the behavior or perception of others through indirect, deceptive, or underhanded tactics, thereby advancing the interests of the manipulator, often at another's expense.

Minimizing: A **coping mechanism** that involves downplaying or reducing the importance of an event or feeling. It's the opposite of exaggerating.

Narcissist: A person whose actions are entirely self-centered and self-serving to the point that their behavior causes major disruption in their own life and trauma to the people in their lives who are closest to them, whether they realize it or not. They are often charismatic, convincing, and can be very charming when they want or need to be. They tend to feel entitled to treat others exactly how they wish because they have a lack of empathy, regard, and remorse for their actions. In short, they want whatever they want, whenever they want and with whomever they want. Many are good with kids and warm a mother's heart, thereby setting the stage for **grooming**.

Narcissistic slap: A cutdown intended to hurt another's self-image and self-esteem, as a form of **manipulation**.

Pedophile: A person who is both sexually and romantically attracted to children.

Post-traumatic stress disorder: A mental health condition that is triggered by a terrifying event. Symptoms may include flashbacks, nightmares, and severe anxiety as well as uncontrollable thoughts of the event.

Rationalizing: A **coping mechanism** that involves attempting to explain or justify one's own or another's behavior with logical, plausible reasons, even when these are not true or appropriate.

Roofied: Being given the drug Rohypnol (sometimes known as the *date-rape drug*) without your knowledge. Signs include extreme drowsiness and even amnesia, meaning the person will not remember what happened during the time they were under the influence, depending on the amount consumed.

Sexual abuse: Any unwanted sexual contact that is afflicted by one person on another.

Shaming: A type of **manipulation** whereby one person makes another feel so guilty that they comply with the abusive behavior. When the Wolf told me I'd be a "bad girl" if I didn't continue to have sex with him, he was shaming me.

Victimization: The act of singling someone out for cruel, unjust, and undeserved treatment.

Further Reading

The Courage to Heal; A Guide to Women Survivors of Child Sexual Abuse by Ellen Bass and Laura Davis

The Body Keeps the Score: Brain, Mind and Body in the Healing of Trauma by Bessel Van Der Kolt

Start Here: A Crash Course in Understanding, Navigating and Healing from Narcissistic Abuse by Dana Morning Star

Happiness Is a Choice by Barry Neil Kaufman

To Love Is to Be Happy With by Barry Neil Kaufman

Hands of Light: A Guide to Healing Through the Human Energy Field by Barbara Ann Brennan

Light Emerging: The Journey of Personal Healing by Barbara Ann Brennan

A Just Forgiveness: Responsible Healing Without Excusing Injustice by Everett L. Worthington Jr.

This song was written by my friend Theresa.
It captures exactly how I feel about God in my life right now.

New Life

New life, God's giving me new life.
New life, God's giving me new life.
There's a seed inside me growing of love that God is sowing.
New life, God's giving me new life.

God's love, God's giving me love.
God's love, God's giving me love.
I can feel forgiveness flowing, as God's love in me is growing.
God's love, God's giving me love.

God's peace, God's giving me peace.
God's peace, God's giving me peace.
There's a quiet place inside me
where a still small voice will guide me
God's peace, God's giving me peace.

God's joy, God's giving me joy.
God's joy, God's giving me joy.
To give one's self completely to God who loves so deeply
is joy, God's giving me joy.

AMBER GREGORY

New life, God's giving me new life.
New life, God's giving me new life.
There's a flame inside me growing of love, I hope it's showing.
New life, God's giving me new life.

Amber Gregory is available to speak in person or virtually.

To contact Amber go to
ambergregoryauthor.com

or email her at
ambergregoryauthor@gmail.com

Song of a Christian Sufi
A Spiritual Memoir

*Grace and grit have truly met and embraced in
the author's unflinchingly honest and compassionate
account of her lifelong journey as a spiritual seeker.*
—Cynthia Bourgeault

This is the story of a woman's spiritual journey: from the restrictions of growing up as Catholic female in the 1950s to her emotional and spiritual liberation as a Sufi—and to her ultimate return to a new understanding of Christianity. Building on the foundations of the Sufi and Christian mystics, Della Penna's memoir is sometimes funny, sometime heartbreaking—and always points toward more universal truths beyond the particularities of an individual life. It will resonate with anyone seeking to find life's deeper meanings. The author's discovery of her own unique "song" is truly a gift to us all!

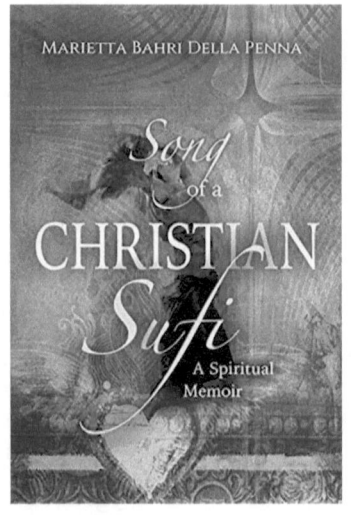

Soul Friendship in the Celtic Tradition
Ancient Insights for Today

The special friend who accompanies a person through life's journey is more precious than gold. The early Christian Celts had a heartwarming name for this person: the Anamchara. (*Anam* is the Gaelic word for soul; *chara* is the word for friend—"friend of the soul.") This special friend was someone with whom a person could talk through practical matters, reveal hidden intimacies, and break through the barriers of convention and egotism to an eternal unity of soul.

Ray Simpson brings this ancient concept into the twenty-first century, drawing practical applications from the long history of soul friendship. He describes a spiritual bond that lasts beyond this life into eternity, for it flows directly from God, who is the pattern of all friendship, the center and source of all human relationships.

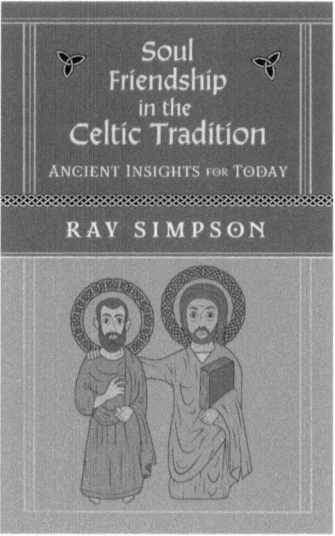

ANAMCHARA BOOKS

www.anamcharabooks.com

www.ingramcontent.com/pod-product-compliance
Lightning Source LLC
Chambersburg PA
CBHW060528080526
44586CB00012B/662